Irisanya Moon's *Circe* provides critical insight into one of the most fascinating characters in Greek mythology. Moon's insights and fresh perspectives in this book make the often-misunderstood Circe relatable and accessible to a wide variety of readers who wish to learn more about one of the first witches of ancient Greece. This book, with its multi-faceted approach and diverse activities, is one I would highly recommend to anyone who wishes to not only learn more about Circe but also to embody their own unique power.

Robin Corak, author of *Persephone* and *Demeter*

This introduction to Circe is a fascinating read. I found it inspiring and challenging - in some really good ways. The book is an invitation to power and magic, and particularly to untame feminine power and magic for resisting oppression. Reading Irisanya's work made me think a lot about the power of anger, and the importance of being able to change yourself, and change direction. It's a small text with a great deal to offer and I can very much recommend it.

Nimue Brown, author of *Beyond Sustainability: Authentic Living at a Time of Climate Crisis*

Be prepared for Irisanya Moon's book *Circe, Goddess of Sorcery* to take you on a wild and entertaining journey through ancient Greece! Here you will meet the enigmatic Circe, goddess of magic and daughter of the sun. This book is a well-crafted and researched guide to working with Her and covers every aspect of her magic, including spell work and necromancy. Irisanya is the perfect teacher to inspire you to have a rich and fulfilling relationship with the goddess Circe.

Thea Prothero, author of *A Guide to Pilgrimage*

Irisanya Moon offers a compelling introduction to an oft-misunderstood yet enthralling figure from the Greek pantheon. The author is careful to take note of biases from certain translations of texts and offers insights from women classicists - which seems completely apt when considering this strong, independent, powerful sorceress born of a Sun God and a Nymph; Fire and Water. This book is an entire journey with Circe, from making space for Her to come into your life to discovering Her history to spellwork and so much more. Circe is fascinating to me, especially in my roles as a devotee of Hekate and a witch, and this book is a fabulous resource blending magic, history, and personal experience. Beyond this, the author has created a timely and relevant book when one considers current conversations about gender power imbalance; a book that makes intelligent insights about perspectives, the nature of evil, and transforming anger into justice.

Mabh Savage, author of *Practically Pagan: An Alternative Guide to Planet Friendly Living*

Pagan Portals
Circe

Goddess of Sorcery

Pagan Portals
Circe

Goddess of Sorcery

Irisanya Moon

MOON
BOOKS
London, UK
Washington, DC, USA

CollectiveInk

First published by Moon Books, 2024
Moon Books is an imprint of Collective Ink Ltd.,
Unit 11, Shepperton House, 89 Shepperton Road, London, N1 3DF
office@collectiveinkbooks.com
www.collectiveinkbooks.com
www.moon-books.net

For distributor details and how to order please visit the 'Ordering' section on our website.

Text copyright: Irisanya Moon 2023

ISBN: 978 1 80341 382 2
978 1 80341 383 9 (ebook)
Library of Congress Control Number: 2023943428

A CIP catalogue record for this book is available from the British Library.

Design: Lapiz Digital Services

UK: Printed and bound by CPI Group (UK) Ltd, Croydon, CR0 4YY
Printed in North America by CPI GPS partners

We operate a distinctive and ethical publishing philosophy in all areas of our business, from our global network of authors to production and worldwide distribution.

Contents

Circe is a feared goddess who used Her knowledge of nature and sorcery to transform those who displeased Her into animals and monsters. Sorceress and enchantress, Circe offers lessons in alchemizing anger into action, of using magick for justice.

Acknowledgments

I want to thank Moon Books for supporting my writing. Not only have I grown as an author, but I'm certain I have grown as a person through feedback, collaboration, and opportunities. Special thanks to Trevor Greenfield for his ongoing encouragement and ability to find places for me to share my thoughts with a wider audience.

I also want to thank my friends, beloveds, and chosen family. I'm ever grateful for those who have walked this weird path with me and heard me obsess about what I'm writing next, and whether it's good enough. My friends inspire me daily to believe in myself and to continue. Without their support, I'm not sure I would still be sitting on my couch, getting to know another deity, and sharing what I think will be helpful.

I acknowledge the godds who have joined me in ways, loud and silent ways. While this book might be about Circe, she was not the only one who joined me in this book's creation. I credit Iris for helping me in the moments when I couldn't figure out what to say or how to say it. And I thank Aphrodite for Her ongoing tending of my heart when I am struggling.

But I thank Circe for calling to me, tapping me on my shoulder, and turning my head in a direction I had avoided. I am sure I am better for it. We moved toward each other slowly, and I am sure the relationship we are creating is one that will have lasting deliciousness.

Author's Note

Having written several Pagan Portals books (*Aphrodite: Encountering the Goddess of Love & Beauty & Initiation, Iris: Goddess of the Rainbow & Messenger of the Godds, Norns: Weavers of Fate & Magick,* and *Artemis: Goddess of the Wild Hunt & Sovereign Hunt*), I realize that some readers have wondered why these books are shorter in length than other books about deities.

The Pagan Portals series is meant to introduce the godds featured. This book, nor any other Pagan Portals books, are meant to be comprehensive. Think of this as a starting point, a place from which you can do your own research, your own relationship-building, and your own magickal journey.

To me, I think of these books as being 'first dates' with deities and mythological figures. You learn a little bit, you see if you feel any stirrings of wanting to know more, and then you can decide whether another date (or more) is something you want to pursue.

I also am clear (and hope you are too) that my insights and offerings come from my personal lens, and as such, you and I, dear reader, may not agree. I am glad for that. I do not think everyone should agree. It's an impossible task. What is possible, even probable, is that in the future, I could change my mind about how I look at something and how I wrote about something. Time does that, offers perspective and depth, thankfully.

As in my other books, here's a note about my spellings and capitalization. Whenever I can, I will capitalize pronouns associated with deities. It's possible (maybe even probable) that will miss one here and there, but I hope I did not.

I also use 'godds' as the spelling for deities to help expand the gender of deities, as I feel godds are beyond gender definitions and standards. To use this slightly different spelling allows for the differentiation from the Christian god.

Finally, the term 'ancient Greece' is one that I will reference in this book, knowing full well that this area was expansive and thus not everyone in that area did all the things that everyone else did. Instead, I use this more as a general term for the time to be consistent and to avoid confusion for a reader.

Introduction

I was first introduced to Circe when I was starting out my witchcraft journey, though I did not realize I would return to Her later. But this meeting wasn't in a trance or a ritual. This meeting was gossip and secondhand stories about a witch named Lady Circe.

What I had heard in the small witchcraft community in Toledo, Ohio, was that Lady Circe was, well, unkind and unforgiving. I had heard she was prone to outrages and was a person you wanted to avoid. She was a high priestess who held power among those practicing witchcraft in that area, but she was not the only one.

There was another witch in the area who told me again and again that Circe was 'trouble,' dangerous, even. Again and again, I heard Lady Circe was someone who would cause harm to those who She didn't agree with. Lady Circe was frightening and vengeful. As a new witch, I listened to this warning. I wasn't at the point in my life of questioning the source of this information.

So, I stayed away. I stayed away from Circe. I crafted in my head a story that She would hurt me somehow. These were times without the internet and the inkling to look someone up to see if the rumors were true.

From what I can tell now, it doesn't seem the stories were completely accurate. Further, the witch who told me to stay away from Lady Circe turned out to be someone who tried to attack me psychically later that year. So, take from that what you will. The one telling the story might have their own motivations for telling it the way they did. (And who among us hasn't done the same? Who is to say I'm not doing that on some level now?)

I share this story because when I later learned about Circe, the Greek goddess, I began to see the story more clearly. This narrative follows many goddesses in the Greek pantheon: those of power are those who are to be feared. Those who took things into their own hands were categorized as evil. And those who are threatened by this power will do all they can to make others question it.

Circe is self-possessed and mighty. And She offers us a way to step into our own power, fully and unapologetically.

What follows is my interpretation and integration of the texts that survive, through the eyes of those who translated the ancient Greek. This means I will likely have interpretations that only resonate with some readers. I bring my own lens into the conversation, and I hope you can consider what resonates for you and contemplate what does not as a starting point for discussion versus argument. We do not have to agree. I am not here to talk you into my point of view.

A few things about translations. Many academics involved in translating texts have been white men, and, as such, this has sometimes led to missing pieces of stories or confusing interpretations across translations. While it can be said translations are educated guesses, and no one translation is the 'true' one, I want to challenge the standard of having a certain set of translators, with similar backgrounds and educations.

To address this, I want to promote the idea of women translators and translations of *The Odyssey*, where Circe has a large role with Odysseus himself.

Among the early-modern women who translated the Classics was Anne Lefébvre Dacier (1654–1720), the first woman to translate The Odyssey from Greek to French and one of the most respected Classicists of her time. Even though she and Alexander Pope (1688–1744) were in a feud at the time of her death, Pope is known to have used Dacier as the foundation for his own influential

English translations of Homer, says Erika Harlitz-Kern in an article for *The Week.*[1]

This is an important point to note as the traditional interpretations have consistently shown women/females as problematic, while often softening the same features in men/male characters.

While Penelope is at home, beset by suitors and thinking her husband dead, she is still expected (after twenty years) to remain faithful to her husband. Odysseus, on the other hand, is given a pass by the gods themselves. In fact, it is part of his heroic deed of saving his shipmates from Circe. As Hermes tells him: "...rush her fast as if to run her through!/ She'll cower in fear and coax you to her bed-/ but don't refuse the goddess' bed, not then, not if/ she's to release your friends and treat you well yourself" (Homer, Fagle translation 300)[2]

More recently, Emily Wilson has gotten credit for being someone who has translated the ancient Greek to English, but even she has pointed out the issue with this:

As the media focuses on Wilson as the "first female translator," there is also the issue of tokenism, where one female translator may somehow represent all of them. "I worry about the way that it can potentially erase all the women," Wilson says. "I personally have learned a huge amount from other female classicists, other Homerists; I don't want it to be presented that I'm the only classicist that matters who's female.[3]

I want to point out this concern about translations to ensure the possibility of critical thinking across any study of Greek mythology (and any mythology or sacred texts). The person who translates will impact the words that arrive on the page.

May we be aware enough to understand how this might directly change or misrepresent the meaning of the words in the original cultural context.

Words have power. Words hold magick. May we consider them carefully, critically, and kindly.

Notes:

1. https://theweek.com/articles/872174/what-happens-when-women-translate-classics#:~:text=Among%20the%20early%2Dmodern%20women,respected%20Classicists%20of%20her%20time.
2. https://heroesjourneyssummer2017.wordpress.com/2017/07/21/the-odyssey-and-the-heros-journey/
3. https://www.34st.com/article/2019/10/emily-wilson-penn-classical-studies-translation-the-odyssey-macarthur-foundation-genius-grant-fellowship#:~:text=Two%20years%20ago%2C%20Penn's%20Classical,Homer's%20The%20Odyssey%20into%20English.

Chapter 1

Encountering Circe

We must let go of the life we have planned, so as to accept
the one that is waiting for us. – Joseph Campbell
Κιρκη Ι Kirkê Ι Circe Ι Hoop Round (kirkoô)

Circe, there is a sound in the name as it slides across my tongue
and teeth. There is an energy that asks me to pay attention, to
take notice, and to watch closely. I am asked to remember this
is a special type of magick, of sorcery. This magick comes from
within, from the deepest levels of the body and heart.

Circe's name is derived from the Greek verb *kirkoô* or "to
secure with rings" or "hoop around," which references the
power of magick to bind. She of the magick to bind, to overcome.
Her name has also been linked to 'falcon.'

"It is the tale of a Goddess 'beautifully alluring, majestic,
and melodic,'" as Johann Heinrich Voss expresses Her Homeric
qualities in his Germanic translation [of *The Odyssey*]. In the
Greek She is 'frighteningly powerful,' having a seductive and
more shrill than melodic song" (Kerényi 6).

The goddess of sorcery (pharmakeia) knew the powers of
transformation, within and without. She holds the power of
necromancy as one who has known, seen, and caused death.
Circe travels the places of the liminal, the spaces between breath
and action. And She also moves quickly when needed, while
arriving exactly as necessary.

What Circe brings about and weaves does not affect the substance;
it leaves the 'minds' of those transformed untouched, and it
remains on the periphery of the real, like the sorceress herself who
lives near the edge of the world, one day's journey on this site of

the outermost location, from Oceanus, from eternal Night, from the house of Hades (Kerényi 17).

Guiley notes how Homer described Circe as 'fair-haired' and that She 'controlled fate and the forces of creation and destruction with braids in her hair' (65). In *The Encyclopedia of Witches and Witchcraft,* Guiley also describes Circe as a moon goddess and a goddess of degrading love.

This is a deity who emerges in stories in moments where She is the best person to help, but then also disappears just as quickly, as though Her impact must be contained. One might say She is the first witch, as there were no words in ancient Greece for 'witch' and no descriptions of such a creature or possibility...until Circe.

Making Space for Circe

Before learning more about Circe, I invite you to make room for Her in your life. This can be a simple promise to spend time in devotion and study with Her. You might also want to create a physical space for Her, like an altar.

You can choose an image of Circe you find, or you might create a place with a piece of paper that includes Her name. This way, you have found a place for Her in your life, a place where your attention can return. A place where your intention can reside, the intention to get to know Her more.

I encourage you to spend just a few minutes with Circe daily or as often as you can remember. This will help you tap into Her energy and start to see the nuances of how She might show up in your life now. Just like any new friend, it's always kind to make space for a new person in your life. This will help you build a strong foundation for whatever relationship comes next.

That said, you may not be reading this book to create a relationship. You may, instead, be looking to just learn more or to supplement your experience with the Circe of other books and media. This is welcome, too, of course.

For Those Who Work with Other Deities

If you are working with other deities right now, you might want to consider letting them know you will be working with Circe right now. This will help you be clear in your relationships with other godds, and you can decide to step back from other devotional practices for a bit if that seems wise or what your other deities.

Or you can be clear about balancing the time you have to build deity practices. I find that putting times on my calendar helps me see if I am balancing my time well. By creating a schedule, it will also keep me honest about when I will focus in certain directions If I miss a time, I will reschedule it, but I try to stick to things I have promised as much as possible.

This will also help me see if a new deity relationship is a good idea. After all, if I can't keep up with the human or divine relationships I have in my life, then I might need to reconsider whether I need to reduce my time with other godds or if I need to find other ways to fit in the magickal work I want to do.

Trance to Meet Circe

To help you start to connect deeper with Circe, I want to offer a trance working. You can choose to read this aloud to a recording device and then play it back, or you can have someone else read it to you. Or you can choose to read it a few times to know it well enough to guide yourself into the space.

Once you have chosen what makes the best sense to you, you will need to set aside some time for this practice. You will want to have a place where you will not be interrupted for about 30 minutes, depending on how quickly you read/follow the trance. It can help to be in a space where there are no loud noises or the potential of a phone ringing.

You will want to find a way for your body to be relaxed, but also aware. While it's not a problem to fall asleep during a trance, if you can stay awake, that seems to be more helpful. You might choose to sit in a way that keeps your back straight, as in a chair or against a wall. Or you might walk around as you listen to the trance (that's what I tend to do). You can also lay down if that feels best for your body. I encourage you to close your eyes if that feels right for you. For some, it will not, so you can choose to keep your eyes slightly open to be aware of your surroundings. You can also choose to keep your eyes open but focused on a flame or a calming item on your altar.

Once you find the right place and space, you will want to notice your breath. You don't need to change it or breathe deeper. You can just follow your breath as it is, noticing how it moves with your body. Allow it to be something that can help you feel grounded and centered. If you find another sound that works better, focus on that in the room. You can also choose to touch the ground or your clothing as a grounding touchpoint if that feels more centering.

As you settle in, we will start by doing a progressive relaxation exercise, helping to settle your entire body and mind, allowing you to be more in the moment. This will take you more deeply into the trance and allow you to gain even more information from the experience. I invite you to take your time with this part, not rushing to finish it to get to the 'good' part. Moving slowly allows you to deepen.

Trance Text (for recording):

I invite you to find a way to settle your body, moving it in the way it needs to move to be most comfortable and at ease. If you need another moment to find this feeling, take that moment. Once you are settled, allow your awareness to drop to the space of your feet and ankles. In this space, just notice what is present and what is happening in these spaces. *There is no need to fix or change anything, just notice. And if there is anything that doesn't need to be there, you can allow it to drop, sink, and fall away from your body.*

(Leave space for silence here.)

Next, allow your awareness to travel to the space of your calves and knees. In these spaces, notice what is present and what is happening. There is no need to fix or change anything, just notice. If there is anything that doesn't need to be there, you can allow it to drop, sink, and fall away from your body.

(Leave space for silence here.)

You can then allow your awareness to travel to the space of your thighs and hip bones, swirling around your pelvic bowl. In these spaces, notice what is present and what is happening. There is no need to fix or change anything, just notice. And if there is anything that doesn't need to be there, you can allow it to drop, sink, and fall away from your body.

(Leave space for silence here.)

Your awareness can now travel to the space of your abdomen and the space of digestion and will. In these spaces, notice what is present at this moment. There is no need to fix or change anything, just notice. If there is anything that doesn't need to be there, you can allow it to drop, sink, and fall away from your body.

(Leave space for silence here.)

Next, allow your awareness to travel to the space of your ribcage, lungs, and heart, that courageous heart. Notice what is present and what is happening. There is no need to fix or change anything, just notice. If there is anything that doesn't need to be there, you can allow it to drop, sink, and fall away from your body.

(Leave space for silence here.)

With ease, your awareness travels to the space of your arms, from collarbones to shoulders, down to elbows, fingers, and thumbs. In these places, notice what is present and what is happening. There is no need to fix or change anything, just notice. If anything doesn't need to be there, you can allow it to drop, sink, and fall away from your body.

(Leave space for silence here.)

As you continue to feel more and more relaxed, your awareness can travel to the space of your throat, jaw, and head, even to the place on top that was soft when you were born. Notice what is present and what is happening. There is no need to fix or change anything, just notice. And if there is anything that doesn't need to be there, you can allow it to drop, sink, and fall away from your body.

(Leave space for silence here.)

In this space of potential and possibility, allow anything else to fall away that doesn't need to be in your body or your mind. You can let it go right now without any resistance. And you can know that if there is anything you need to pick up again, it will be waiting for you when you complete this work.

From this space and place, you can allow your awareness to open and unfurl like a blanket, like a rose, like each fluffy pappus from a dandelion. Allow your awareness to spread out to the horizon. You might experience this as a vision or as a sense that things are widening and opening before you. At all times, you're in control of this experience, and you can stop if needed or you can come back to your breath to deepen further.

As things open and unfurl and unfold, you will begin to see or feel things sharpen into a place with a path. This path might lead you to an island, or it might be a part of an island, or it might be another place that seems right for you. No matter what you notice or sense at this point, I invite you to follow the path laid out before you.

I invite you to open your senses as you travel this path. What do you see or sense? What do you notice or experience? What becomes clearer with each step? What does your body feel like? What do you notice in terms of temperature or texture? What happens as you continue to move toward an unknown place? Are there colors? Are there seasons? Are there tight places or a loosening?

At some point, you may begin to be aware of an energy, a presence. Allow yourself to notice what this feels like for you. Can you begin to feel the sensation that you are not alone? That this place has someone who is waiting for you, who has been waiting for you to arrive? Take the time you need to drop into this space and know the energy can be subtle and know you can trust what you feel.

(Leave a few moments of silence to arrive in this space.)

This energy is Circe greeting you in Her home. She has been waiting for you, waiting for you to arrive. She welcomes you to the space and assures you of your safety. She might take time to show you around or you might sit down with Her and start to talk. Or you might get a sense that She is present in more of an energetic way. No matter how you experience this moment, take a few minutes to be with Her and see what arises.

Does She have wisdom to share? Do you have questions to ask? Does She offer you anything? What happens when you get a chance to finally meet?

(Wait a few minutes before speaking again.)

Once you have spent the time you need here, it's wise to thank Her for Her time. You can remind yourself that you are able to return to this space again if you like. But for this moment, you will return to your body by finding your way back the same way you arrived.

Again, be sure to thank Circe, or whoever showed up. Offer Her a gift or take what She gives you before you turn and find the path again. Find that path you traveled and move back the way you came. You might notice different things this time. You might notice new things. You might see things as being brighter or clearer. Or you might not see anything different. Your unique experience is just right.

Follow the path to the place where you unfolded and unfurled your awareness. Bring it back into your body where it can be right-sized for everyday living. You do not need to be that expanded all the time. Once that is folded and tucked back in, you can find your awareness traveling back down your body, becoming more and more present.

Coming back to your head, your jaw, and your throat, coming back.
Back to your collarbones, shoulders, elbows, fingers, and thumbs, coming back.
Back to your courageous heart, lungs, and ribcage, coming back.
Back to your will, place of digestion, and abdomen, coming back.
Back to your pelvic bowl, hips, and thighs, coming back.
Back to your knees, calves, ankles, and feet, coming back.

Coming back and opening your eyes if they have been closed. Shake your body and run your hands along your arms and thighs. You might say your name aloud a few times to bring yourself back into this moment. I will often say something that is very mundane, like my address or my phone number. This way, I know my brain is back in the present day.

Afterward, you can also choose to journal about your experience. This can help you begin to collect pieces of information, even if they don't quite make sense yet. Keep track of what you felt, what you saw or sensed, and what you left knowing from Circe.

Meeting a deity can be an intense experience, and it can also offer you a more personal connection. From the start of any relationship, taking time to experience what the other being has to offer can be highly informative. I know I personally prefer to meet deities where they already reside in me versus learning what others have said about them first. Let Circe tell you what She thinks you need to know for now.

And if you didn't have the experience you expected, know this is okay too. You can always return to this practice later. Sometimes, it takes a few tries to connect, but if you are committed, future attempts are appreciated by the one you seek.

Chapter 2

Circe's Family & Companions

Soon Dawn appeared and touched the sky with roses.
    The Odyssey, translated by Emily Wilson

While many of us had to read *The Odyssey* during our school years, I can imagine most of us did not look at it that closely. And even fewer of us remembered the poetry of the journey and how it was one of courage and cunning. Circe arrives in the list of godds at the start of *Theogony*, but later in the story of Odysseus.

Parents & Siblings

Kirke (Circe), a goddess with braided hair, with human speech and with strange powers; baleful Aeetes was her brother, and both were radiant Helios the sun-god's children; their mother was Perse, Okeanos' (Oceanus') daughter. (Homer, Odyssey 10. 135 ff, trans. Shewring)

The parents of Circe are said to be Helios (the Sun) and Perse (a nymph born of Oceanus). Some translations, however, offer that Circe's mother may have been Hecate, who may have conceived Her with Aeëtes.

Within these possible parent pairings, Circe is said to have a few siblings: Aeëtes, Pasiphaë, and Perses with Helios and Perse, and Medea with Hecate and Aeëtes. Circe's siblings have their own stories and complications.

Aeëtes – this brother of Circe is one She is very close to, and She loves him very much.

Pasiphaë – this sister of Circe is the Queen of Crete, and also known as a goddess of witchcraft and sorcery; she is also described as being the one who birthed the Minotaur.

Perses – also known as the 'destroyer,' this brother of Circe is not to be confused with the Titan named Perses, who fathered Hecate.

Medea – known as a sorceress and witch, as well as a priestess of Hecate, Medea features in the story of Jason and Argonauts, helping him find the Golden Fleece.

Partners

The main story of Circe involves Odysseus finding Her on Her island, where he ends up staying for a year. Odysseus is a being who has talents from the time he is young, talents that will make him a great leader. Not only does he try to gain the hand of Helen of Troy, but he also marries the cunning Penelope and pretends to be crazy not to help Helen's husband during the war. (This is just a small glimpse into the soap opera that Greek mythology offer offers.) Odysseus fought in the Trojan War alongside Achilles, playing an instrumental role in communicating with the right people to gain favorable outcomes.

Circe also partnered with Telemachus, the son of Odysseus and Penelope. In *Telegony*, a book that outlines and describes what happens after Odysseus returns from his journey, including his accidental death, Telemachus returns to Aeaea, where he marries Circe.

Telemachus is often discussed in *The Odyssey* as the son who was always looking for his father, Odysseus. And in the end, Telemachus returns from the epic journey before his father.

Children

During the time that Odysseus and Circe were together, they conceived at least three children, with sources including the following names as part of the sibling group:

Latinus – son of Circe and Odysseus, who ruled over the Tyrrhenians.

Telegonus – son of Circe and Odysseus, who ruled over the Tyrrhenians; the one who accidentally killed Odysseus with a lance dipped in the poisonous spine of a stingray.

Ardeas – son of Circe and Odysseus, who ruled over the Tyrrhenians.

Rhomos – son of Circe and Odysseus, who is said to have founded the city of Rome.

Anteias – son of Circe and Odysseus, is said to have founded the city of Anteia.

Nymphs of Aeaea

[In the home of the witch Kirke (Circe):] Four handmaids of hers were busying themselves about the palace. She has them for her household tasks, and they come from springs (krênai) [i.e., Nymphai Krenaides], they come from groves (alsea) [i.e. Nymphai Alseides], they come from the sacred rivers (potamoi) flowing seawards [i.e. Nymphai Potameides]. One spread the chairs with fine crimson covers above and with linen cloths beneath; in front of the chairs, a second drew up silver tables on which she laid gold baskets for bread; a third mixed honey-sweet lovely wine in a silver bowl sand set the golden goblets out; the fourth brought water and lit a great

fire under a massive cauldron. The water warmed; and when it boiled in the bright bronze vessel, the goddess made me [Odysseus] (Homer, Odyssey 10. 348 ff, trans. Shewring)

At various storytelling points, nymphs show up on the island of Circe, helping to feed and honor guests. These nymphs act as handmaidens and servants, preparing spaces for those who entered the halls, even if they were to be turned into pigs and other animals.

In having nymphs attend to Her needs, Circe focuses directly on those who would enter Her hall and ask Her for favors, spells, and mercy.

Chapter 3

Circe Stories & Myths

Tell me about a complicated man.
Muse, tell me how he wandered and was lost
when he had wrecked the holy town of Troy,
and where he went, and who he met, the pain
he suffered in the storms at sea, and how
he worked to save his life and bring his men
back home. He failed to keep them safe; poor fools,
they ate the Sun God's cattle, and the god
kept them from home. Now goddess, child of Zeus,
tell the old story for our modern times.
Find the beginning.
(Emily Wilson, The Odyssey)

When getting to know a godd like Circe, it can help to see the kinds of stories told about Her. This doesn't mean all these stories are accurate or helpful to know, but they offer pieces in the puzzle that make up the complexity of Circe.

How Circe Came to the Isle of Aeaea (Aiaia)

Apollonios (Apollonius), following Hesiod, says that Kirke (Circe)
came to the island over against Tyrrhenia on the chariot of Helios.
And he called it Hesperian, because it lies towards the west.
(Hesiod, Catalogues of Women Fragment 46, trans. Evelyn-White)

Circe lived on the island of Aeaea (or Aiaia), also called the Island of the Dawn, with some stories describing the way She was exiled to the mythical place by Her father after Circe killed Her husband and turned a romantic rival into Scylla, a sea monster. Translations speak of Her being taken to the island by the golden chariot of Her father, Helios.

Monaghan states:

> ...this illustrious witch was said to have gained the rulership of Colchis near the Black Sea by marrying its prince. Then she killed him so that she could rule alone. When Circe's subjects discovered her crime, they rose gainst her. The enchantress fled, escaping her father's rays to the island of Aeaea (88).

Sources also describe how Circe was brought to the island by dragons, not necessarily by force. In other stories, there seems to be a conversation between Aphrodite and Medea, with Aphrodite in disguise as Circe. 'Circe' in this conversation talks about not liking Her father's land, so it is possible that Circe simply left to find a better place to inhabit. While Madeline Miller's *Circe* speaks of the dramatic exile by Helios, this might be a storytelling device also to give more rationale for Circe's eventual actions and reactions.

No matter how Circe came to be on the island of Aeaea, the mythical and magickal place became Her home. This wild and densely forested place was the home of men who were turned into animals (lions and wolves). In *The Odyssey*, the island also includes wide areas of pasture for animals, as well as high bluffs from which the sea could be seen in all directions.

While it is not clear where this island was located, there is speculation that Aeaea would have been an island off the coast of Italy. On the island, Circe lived in a grand stone house, so hidden by the dense forests that it could not be easily seen or discovered.

Odysseus

[Odysseus] hastened to tie the cunning knot which Lady Kirke (Circe) had brought to his knowledge in other days. (Homer, Odyssey 8. 447 ff)

In *The Odyssey*, Odysseus makes his way to the island of Circe, knowing a goddess with braided hair and human speech lived there. It was rumored She had strange, even magickal powers, for Her family also had special talents for sorcery. Weary from the journey, Odysseus and his men found a place to shelter their boat, staying on the island's shore for two days.

On the third day, Odysseus traveled out from the boat, hoping to find human contact and food for his men, but finding none, he started to return to the boat and came upon a stag that he killed for food. As the dawn rose, Odysseus gathered all his men to explore the island to see what they could use or find. At that time, it was unclear if the island had any inhabitants, but smoke rose from the dense woodland, hinting at the presence of someone or something.

The men were afraid, having already known of the Cyclops and other monsters during their journey. They worried for their lives, and they cried out in fear. But Odysseus put them into groups and moved to the island to see what they could find. Soon, they came upon the stone palace of Circe, surrounded by entranced animals who greeted the men. This confused the soldiers, who could also hear the song of Circe from within. The men followed the sound, thinking the group of men would be more effective and powerful in their numbers.

Circe called the men into Her palace, though one soldier stayed outside, fearing the worst. But She was kind, and they were hungry. She offered them a cheese and barley meal with honey and wine. What the men did not know was the potion Circe had added to the food, so they ate until they had their fill. But in doing so, they were turned into pigs, from snout to bristles.

The one man, Eurylokhos, who did not enter, ran back to the ship to tell of the horror. But he could not speak, as he was so sad about the outcome of the other men. In response, Odysseus put his sword on his back and gathered his bow to prepare to fight Circe and get his men back. The man who survived was less than thrilled to return to Circe and begged Odysseus to stay. But Odysseus knew he had to go, leaving the weeping man at the ship.

At the door of Circe's house, Odysseus met with Hermes, who also warned him of entering the place and how he would be turned into a swine. Hermes offered to help Odysseus by giving him a magick herb of virtue to offer to Circe for Her to make a potion. This potion would make it so Circe would be unable to enchant him, and even more, the potion would cause Her to shrink back if Odysseus were to rush Her with a sword. Hermes then told Odysseus to lay with Circe as that will help to release his men. But it was important for Odysseus to have Circe swear the great oath of the Blessed Ones to plot no mischief in the days after.

The events transpired just as Hermes described, causing Circe to be confused by Her position not working as it should have – and always had – and to offer to have Odysseus lie with Her in Her bed, with an acknowledgment that they needed to trust each other. At his request, Circe uttered the oath, and they lay together.

During this time, handmaidens moved through the palace, cleaning and preparing food. Odysseus was dressed in a fine robe after a bath. A delicious meal was laid out before him, but he was unhappy and would not eat. She asked him why, and he admitted he was unsure he could trust Her, even though She had sworn the oath. After all, he had seen his men be turned into animals. Odysseus asked to see his men, and Circe brought them into the room in the shape of swine. She anointed them all one by one with a charm, turning them back into the form of men.

In seeing the men reunited in joy and contentment, Circe offered them compassion and told Odysseus to bring the rest of the men from the ship to the palace. The men were overjoyed to see Odysseus again and to find out their friends were safe. They were more than happy to return to the palace, where there was plenty of food and drink.

Once again, Eurylokhos hesitated and didn't want to go back into the possibility of danger, but eventually, he agreed to go, following the will of Odysseus. They were greeted by Circe and the men, who had been dressed, anointed, and fed. This was the way of the group in Circe's palace for a year, with Circe insisting they stay and regain the strength they lost in the previous journey.

At the end of the year, Circe made good on Her promise to help the men return home. As Circe did not want Odysseus and the others to stay out of spite and not desire, She instructed them to follow the way to the house of Persephone and Hades. Circe promised Odysseus that She would help him get to where he needed to go.

While Odysseus traveled and returned from the underworld unharmed, he returned to Circe. She let him know how to bypass the Sirens he would find on the way back. And in doing so, Circe allowed Odysseus to return from his 20-year voyage.

A reader may want to take note the response of Penelope upon the return of Odysseus and how she waited for him and remained faithful and likely was expected to remain faithful.

What else does Penelope expect (and get) from Odysseus? First of all, proof that she is in her way as important to him as he is to her.

She does not demand strict fidelity; she and Helen do not object to their husbands' liaisons with other women, so long as they are temperate; Odysseus tells Penelope about Circe and Calypso (Lefkowitz 125).

How Circe behaves also seems to align with other actions of goddesses in the Greek myths, as these myths have been translated. "The mature goddesses are less helpful to men than the virgins [goddesses]. Like Calypso and Circe, they're more likely to detain a hero through their sexual magic" (Pomeroy 10).

Jason & Medea

In the story of Jason and Medea, Circe had a dream that shook Her from sleep, but She realized it did not hold power over Her when She awoke. The dream was filled with visions of blood coming into Her house, which seemed unlikely. But soon, She was confronted by the dream's meaning, as dreams always seem to have meaning for the godds.

She [Circe] had been terrified by a nightmare in which she saw all the rooms and walls of her house streaming with blood, and fire devouring all the magic drugs with which she used to bewitch her visitors. But she managed to put out the red flames with the blood of a murdered man, gathering it up in her hands; and so the horror passed. When morning came she rose from bed, and now she was washing her hair and clothes in the sea. A number of creatures whose ill-assorted limbs declared them to be neither man nor beast had gathered round her like a great flock of sheep following their shepherd from the fold...The Argonauts were dumbfounded by the scene. (Apollonius Rhodius, Argonautica 4. 662 ff)

Jason and Medea came to Circe's home, asking for refuge, which Circe realized was a request to be hidden because of a murder Jason committed on his journey. While Circe offered

23

them hospitality and food, She tried to purify them for what has happened. After realizing what had happened with Medea, a blood relative cursed to never return home unless Circe purifies Her, Circe did not offer them any more support once the purification is done.

'Poor girl,' she said, 'you have indeed contrived for yourself a shameful and unhappy homecoming; for I am sure you will not long be able to escape your father's wrath. The wrongs you have done are intolerable, and he will soon be in Hellas to avenge his son's murder. However, since you are my suppliant and kinswoman, I will not add to your afflictions now that you are here. But I do demand that you should leave my house, you that have linked yourself to this foreigner, whoever he may be, this man of mystery whom you have chosen without your father's consent. And do not kneel to me at my hearth, for I never will approve your conduct and your disgraceful flight.' (Apollonius Rhodius, Argonautica 4. 662 ff)

It's interesting to note how Circe seems to be willing to help up to a point, as She knows She has the powers that others need to move on in their lives. I find it strange that Circe continues to be this person, as though She signed up for a life of service, but that is not how She is portrayed in the books. Translations make it seem as though Circe just wanted to be alone, and people kept coming up to Her to ask for things.

If I look at it like that, I can see why She responded the way She did. After all, if She just wanted Her own space, it would be frustrating to be interrupted by people who seem to keep getting into trouble only She can help.

The Death of Odysseus

That sting [of the sting-ray] it was which his mother Kirke (Circe), skilled in many drugs, gave of old to Telegonos (Telegonus) for

24

his long hilted spear, that he might array for his foe's death from the sea. And he beached his ship on the island that pastured goats; and he knew not that he was harrying the flocks of his own father, and on his aged sire who came to the rescue, even on him whom he was seeking, he brought an evil fate. There the cunning Odysseus, who had passed through countless woes of the sea in his laborious adventures, the grievous Sting-ray slew with one blow. (Oppian, Halieutica 2. 497 ff, trans. Mair)

Telegonos, the son of Circe and Odysseus, was a child of many talents was sadly also the one who killed his father accidentally. In some tellings of the tale, Odysseus found out ahead of time from an oracle that he would die at the hand of his son. Because of this, Odysseus did not let his son into his palace, but when he heard the commotion caused by Telegonos not being able to get in the door, Odysseus rushed out, thinking it was Telemachus, only to be struck and killed by his son. Telegonos took his father's body back to Penelope, Odysseus' wife, and then decided to marry his father's wife.

This death happens after Odysseus has left Circe on Her island, after he gets help from Circe to return home safely after 20 years of journeying. I wonder if Circe did not help out if Odysseus might have avoided this fate, even though the oracle prophesied it. And it might be curious to think about whether Circe knew this fate was coming, so that's why She helped Odysseus return home. Again, these are only questions that arrive for me when there are powerful godds getting into trouble that seems avoidable in some ways.

Glaucus & Scylla

I often make the joke that Greek mythology is the place of melodrama, where the godds are so very human in their emotions and actions. In the story of Scylla, a water nymph, and Glaucus, a blue-eyed prince. Glaucus tried to woo Scylla, but

Scylla rebuffed his attempts. Angry at Scylla, Glaucus came to Circe to get help, to help Scylla feel as badly about the loss of love as he does. He asked the great sorceress for a love potion, which She refused to make. Some sources state that Circe herself was "ready to make love anytime day or night, noon or evening. She was reputedly a highly sexed temptress whom Aphrodite had too richly endowed with femininity" (Goodrich 161–162).

He met her then and, mutual greetings given, 'Goddess,' he said, 'Have pity on a god, I beg of you. For you alone Titanis can ease this love of mine, if only I am worthy. No one knows better than I the power of herbs, for I was changed by herbs. And I would have you learn my passion's cause: on the Italian coast, facing Messenia's battlements, I saw Scylla. I blush to tell my wooing words, my promises, my prayers— she scorned them all. But you, let now your magic lips, if spells have aught of sovereignty, pronounce a spell, or if your herbs have surer power, let herbs of proven virtue do their work and win. I crave no cure, nor want my wounds made well; pain need not pass; but make her share my hell!' (Ovid, Metamorphoses 14. 1 ff, trans. Melville)

Circe loved Glaucus too and offered Herself because that would be the better solution than to create a potion, which Glaucus turned down, so She decided to poison Scylla, which turned Scylla's bottom half into rabid dogs and gave her monstrous features. Scylla was so mad at this transformation that she attacked Odysseus and his men during their journey. Glaucus wept when he found out what happened to Scylla.

Circe's anger caused Her to lash out and do horrible things to others who might want what She wants. While it is understandable, the fact that She doesn't do anything to Glaucus directly is an interesting choice. Why didn't She do anything to the one who did not return Her advances? What held Her back from this? To me, how Circe is written off as the jealous woman versus blaming the man for his actions seems to be an example of how a male translator may have seen the story. And to be fair, the original story writer may have created this story in this tone for the same reason, as ancient Greece may have prioritized the man's experience.

Calchus

The story of Kalkhos (Calchus) the Daunian [region in southern Italy] was greatly in love with Kirke (Circe), the same to whom Odysseus came. He handed over to her his kingship over the Daunians and employed all possible blandishments to gain her love; but she felt a passion for Odysseus, who was then with her, and loathed Kalkhos and forbade him to land on her island. However, he would not stop coming, and could talk of nothing but Kirke, and she, being extremely angry with him, laid a snare for him and had no sooner invited him into her palace but she set before him a table covered with all manner of dainties. But the meats were full of magical drugs, and as soon as Kalkhos had eaten of them, he was stricken mad, and she drove him into the pig-styles. After a certain time, however, the Daunians' army landed on the island to look for Kalkhos; and she then released him from the enchantment, first binding him by oath that he would never set foot on the island again, either to woo her or for any other purpose. (Parthenius, Love Romances 12 trans. Gaselee)

Once more, Circe found herself with a male suitor, but one She did not want and did not love, even though Kalkhos did all that he could to win Her favor. Circe was passionate about Odysseus, and the attempts to woo her made Her mad enough to poison Kalkhos with drug-filled meat. This poison turned Kalkhos into a pig for a while, until Circe decided to free him, but only after making sure he could not come back to the island ever again.

One could see this story as one in which Circe is clear about what She wants and will not be deterred by Her desires. And one could also see this story as an overreaction to the advances of another. Or it could be seen as Circe being committed to one person. No matter the explanation, it is clear that Circe can be dangerous when She feels She is being threatened and when Her desires are being threatened.

Picus

Later in Ovid's *Metamorphosis* as translated by Melville, there comes the story of Picus. Picus was a king and the son of Cronus/Kronos. He was a ruler who was beloved by the Numina Fontana (Fountain-Sprites) and Naiads (female spirits or nymphs), and who was wed to Canens, the daughter of Janus.

Picus made the decision to travel to the country to hunt the boars, dressed in a purple cloak with a gold clasp. These woods were also the place where Circe found and harvested herbs for Her potions. On this day, She saw Picus from behind some branches and fell in love with him, with the story describing Circe as dropping the herbs She had collected when Her eyes found him.

The warmth of desire crept into Circe; She wanted to be with Picus, but he was so fast on his horse. However, She would not be deterred and used Her magick to conjure the specter of a boar. The boar ran around the countryside and caught Picus' eye but traveled into a thick of trees where a horse could not follow, leaving Picus on his own in the hidden space.

The heavens began to darken as Circe prayed and chanted and called to the moon to become eclipsed and for fog to cover the land. In this blackness, even the guards of the King Picus were unable to find him. Circe decided to tell Picus how much she was struck by his beauty and his eyes. In this translation, Circe went so far as to kneel before him and beg him to accept her as his.

But Picus was repulsed and told Her that his heart was promised to his wife. He described the depth of his loyalty while

Circe continued to plead for his love and attention. Realizing Her efforts were in vain, She turned to magick to get what She wanted. Using Her wand, turning it west and east, She repeated a spell and turned Picus into a bird. He realized something was wrong as he tried to flee. He felt his body sprouting wings, which is what happened as the spell of Circe took hold.

His purple cloak was now purple wings. His golden clasp became feathers around his throat. Picus' men could not find their king as he was now a woodpecker (Picus is a Latin word for woodpecker), small and quick. While the fog and darkness dissipated, the king's men became outraged and charged at Circe.

Circe called to the godds of Night and sprinkled poison and potions around Her. She reached out to Hecate with Her cries. The woods began to widen, the bushes made noises, and black snakes slithered on the ground as ghosts filled the air. The men were terrified and froze in their places. Circe walked up to the men to touch them with Her poisoned wand, and they became the shape of wild beasts.

Picus was never found again, and his wife died from grief after roaming the countryside to find her husband, and never finding him.

The stories of the godds can help you better understand where their energies and talents come from, while also offering insights into their faults. I know I am often drawn to deities who have flaws and have made mistakes. After all, if I am to believe I am divine too, with flaws and many mistakes, it is comforting to see that the godds have the same.

Chapter 4

Spellwork & Circe

[Invocation to Kirke (Circe):] Daughter of Helios, Kirke the witch (polypharmake), come cast cruel spells; hurt both these men and their handiwork. (Homer's Epigrams 14 trans. Shewring)

Circe is often described as a being of power and magick. Many are drawn to Circe for these reasons, as She appears to be one of the first witches in ancient Greece. And when someone is one of the first of anything, they become an important source of inspiration. While Her actions often inspired by anger and rage, Her spells work and Her potions have caused men to learn their lessons. (This book does not advise turning men into pigs, even if they, or any other person might, seem to deserve it.)

In this section, we will consider what Circe used in Her magick and translate this to the modern world so you can practice sorcery with this sorceress. Her spellwork spans charms, potions, transmutation, and illusion, as well as necromancy, which gives you a wide variety of possible magickal practices.

Though this book is not comprehensive, the following will give you some actionable and straightforward practices you can use today.

Charms & Potions

[Medea] said [to the Argonauts] that she had brought with her many drugs of marvellous potency which had been discovered by her mother Hekate (Hecate) and by her sister Kirke (Circe); and though before this time she had never used them to destroy human beings, on this occasion she would be means of them easily

wreak vengeance upon men who were deserving of punishment. (Diodorus Siculus, Library of History 4. 50. 6)

NOTE: I recommend working closely with an herbalist or an experienced plant medicine practitioner to grow your herbal experience. While this book will cover a few basic practices, it is not meant to be a comprehensive manual on creating healing and/or harmful potions. I recommend starting with information from Rachel Patterson, Amy Blackthorn, Seraphina Capranos, and other experts in your local area.

Throughout the stories of Circe, we hear of Her making potions that will help to turn men into animals. We also hear of how She anoints animals to turn them back into their human form. What we don't hear are the exact recipes for these sorts of magickal workings.

Meanwhile, Procris could not bear to stay in Athens, her desertion being the subject of general gossip, and therefore came to Crete, where Minos found her no more difficult to seduce than had the supposed Pteleon. He bribed her with a hound that never failed to catch his quarry, and a dart that never missed its mark, both of which had been given him by Artemis. Procris, being an ardent huntress, gladly accepted these, but insisted Minos should take a prophylactic draught – a decoction of magical roots invented by the witch Circe – to prevent him from filling her with reptiles and insects. This draught had the desired effect (Graves 299–300)

What we can surmise is the use of herbs and ingredients from ancient Greece. But just because this is what may have been used, we live in modern times, so it makes sense to use what is now available. I found one source mention mandrake, peony, snowdrop, yarrow, poppy, and rue.

The Greek Herbalist[1] outlines the specifics of herbs used in ancient Greece as well as today, which will help you begin to gather the ingredients you might use.

Oregano (Latin name: Origanum vulgare hirtum) – happiness, happy marriage, immune system, antimicrobial, white cell production, heart health, bone strength

Tsai Tou Vounou (Sideritis) – wound care, immune system support, digestion, cold prevention

Lemon Balm (Melissa officinalis) – heart calming, anxiety, depression, insomnia, panic attacks, antiviral

Bay Leaf (Laurus nobilis L.) – protection from disease and evil spirits, trance state induction (at high doses), digestion, cold and fever fighting, arthritis pain and swelling, heart disease risk

St. John's Wort (Hypericum perforatum L.) – cure curses and demons, anxiety, depression, inflammation, bruises, swelling, neuralgic pain, antiviral (check with healthcare providers before using if you're on prescription medications)

Mastic Tree (Pistacia lentiscus) – digestive health, oral health, anti-inflammatory, anti-fungal, nerve repair, wound healing, blood disorders

Sage (Salvia officinalis) – protection from evil, wisdom enhancing, fertility; digestion, snake bite topically, antiseptic, kidneys; bladder, menstrual flow, hernias, bruises, coughs

To align with the energy of Circe and the powerful ways She interacts with the world, I would encourage you to think about herbs that:

- Change perception, e.g., mugwort
- Increase dreaming, e.g., mugwort
- Enhance calm, e.g., chamomile, lavender, etc.
- Taste good

When learning about any ingredients or resources, it can help to approach these interactions like building a relationship with a person or deity. Start by finding herbs and plants you want to learn more about. Then you can try each plant to see how it feels to you and how it makes you feel when you use it or taste it (assuming it is edible).

It can also be a good idea to learn about the herbs around the place you live. This can help connect you more deeply to the location of your home and use things you already have on hand, just as Circe would have.

Spend time looking in your cupboards too to see if there are herbs you might like. You don't have to spend money if you don't want to or can't spare the expense. You might also think about growing herbs you want to use in larger amounts.

ANOTHER NOTE: Make sure you use herbs that are not considered traditional medicine of indigenous groups, e.g., white sage, unless you have the permission of those groups. There are plenty of herbs and plants in your local area that can be suitable, and you can also investigate the herbs and plants of your ancestry to see what might resonate more closely with your individual history.

How to Choose Herbs to Use

In thinking about the properties of the herbs, you can begin to see how Circe herself may have chosen the herbs She chose. While it is clear She was somehow inherently wise in Her herbalism, you can also tap into your intuition to guide you.

- Tap into intention
- Have safe ingredients
- Practice and try
- Use externally

Start by thinking about the intention, as this can be the best way to start the building of energy for the spell working. You can think about what you want the herbs to do and what you want to see in the end. Taking the time to see what you want and why you want it can help you better understand the selection of herbs and other spell steps.

Some will want to write down the intention to remember it and to focus on it more consistently. Or you might chant it over the herbs you use or when you stir them into the liquid or other ingredients. You can also breathe the intention into the spell working by literally breathing into the potion. Others might want to say it aloud at the end when raising energy.

While Circe did not choose herbs based on their safety necessarily, She did choose herbs so certain things would happen. If She did not choose correctly, the potions would not come out the way She wanted them to. If Circe didn't want people to die, She would need to choose certain ingredients over others.

In your practice, I would advise using safe ingredients that can likely be ingested by anyone. The more you choose safe herbs, the more you can play with them and see how they might impact your spell workings. Plus, you can focus on the intention and the practice versus worrying whether you are causing harm inadvertently.

But the key to any magickal practice is this: practice. This means finding different possible combinations of herbs with different mediums (e.g., water, oil, etc.) and seeing how they work. Using a journal would be ideal to document what happens when you use this ingredient over other ingredients. Each time you try a new recipe, write down what you used, how much, what time of day, what moon cycle, what preparation, the intention, and the result.

The more you detail what has happened, the more easily you can see what worked and what might need to change the next time. You can shift things and come up with your recipes. And if you have friends willing to try things out, that can be good information too. While they might have different reactions, the information, and their feedback can steer things in better directions.

What You Might Make

But what can you do with these ingredients? I find this question can slow down the process of becoming a sorcerer. Instead of focusing so much on what the perfect answer is (because there is no one 'right' answer), I encourage you to think about what you are trying to do and what makes sense.

For example, if you are making something to protect, it could be a spray you can use in the air or a powder you put around a place. You can create incense that you burn when you feel extra support, or you can place the mix on the ground where an unwanted person is likely to be. You can create calming teas, helping to soothe a situation or person. You could add sugar to things to help sweeten situations and increase energy.

You could investigate different preparations of herbs to better understand their complexity and how these might support your workings. Here are some that are approachable and accessible for those newer to potion-making.

- **Tinctures** – preparations in alcohol or sugar water with herbs/ingredients in a carrier base
- **Powders** – ground-up mixtures of herbs and dried plants, as well as possibly other ingredients
- **Oils** – concentrated liquids of ingredients either pressed from plant matter or carrier oils with herbs/plants added until infused and then removed
- **Hydrosols** – a distillation of plants and flowers to create a water-based preparation
- **Bath mixtures** – mixtures of herbs and ingredients to be used during a bath
- **Simmering mixes** – mixtures of herbs and ingredients to be simmered in a pot on the stove, infusing the air and environment with intentions
- **Essences** – a less measured approach that can take ingredients, place them into water or other bases, left there for a while, and then the matter is removed, leaving a water essence
- **Tea** – you can make teas with edible ingredients
- **Incense** – grinding up ingredients into a powder will help create an incense that can be burned
- **Food** – it might also be wise to infuse foods with ingredients to support certain intentions and magickal workings

That said, you could also buy things prepared by others to support their work. I think this is a fine option, and it can also be very powerful to try to make your mixes. And even if you can't make your own, adding another ingredient to a mix can help infuse a preparation with your energy.

As a final note before you go off to create new mixes and find plants to support your charms and potions, remember that it's best to source from ethical retailers, those who are not damaging the environment by over-harvesting or using plants not meant for certain groups to use. Find sellers committed to maintaining plant resources; if you're not sure, you can always ask how they ensure plants aren't being over-harvested. You can also ask how things are harvested to ensure better working practices and conditions for staff harvesting.

Transmutation & Illusion

It was not my fault, these animals / who could no longer touch me / through
the rinds of their hardening skins (Margaret Atwood, *Circe/Mud Poems*)

Circe is skilled in turning something into something else (see the many pigs on Her island). She did this out of protection, understandably, and likely to showcase Her skills to prevent future issues. Most sources talk about how She made a potion to make this happen.

The art of transmutation is shifting one thing to another or another state of being. By this definition, freezing and thawing water is transmutation. Or you could say that ingredients of a cake turn into something you can eat versus things in separate containers. If you want to tap into the transmutation magick of Circe, think about what you want to change in your life. Thinking about the state of water can be a helpful visual and practice.

For example, if you want something to become less rigid or slow, you might put that situation's energy into an ice cube and set the intention that things will become less rigid as the ice melts on your altar. Or you might increase the form and rigidity of a vague idea by putting a bowl of intention-filled water into your freezer. Add in a few herbs to enhance the working.

[Medea] entered the palace [of King Kreon (Creon) of Korinthos (Corinth)] by night, having altered her appearance by means of drugs, and set fire to the building by applying to it a little root which had been discovered by her sister Kirke (Circe) and had the property that when once it was kindled it was hard to put out. (Diodorus Siculus, Library of History 4. 54. 5)

Who hasn't wanted to use magick and spells to change how they look or appear to others? From the scene in *The Craft* movie where Sarah changes her hair color, I know I wanted to figure that out for myself as it would be much cheaper than going to a hair salon. However, I have not figured that out. But what I have found is that I do have the power to change how others see me (e.g., glamour magick) and how others perceive me (personal work).

Some easy glamour magick ideas include:

- Putting on a new piece of jewelry charged with the energy I want to embody
- Setting an intention in a cord or ribbon and wearing it until the spell is complete
- Adding a new clothing piece that makes me feel happy, powerful, etc.
- Wearing certain colors for certain purposes
- Using makeup to change my energy for ritual, e.g., certain designs for certain deities or types of workings (runes, for example)

- Writing my intention or desired energy on a piece of paper and placing it in my shoe while I walk into a certain situation

And as for personal work, you can change how others interact with you (because you are changing how you interact with them). Personal work is, well, personal, but I can offer a few ideas that can inspire you to find something that works for you.

Use **affirmations** to remind yourself of your power, e.g., I am powerful. I am resilient. I am worthy of respect. I am unstoppable. I have good ideas. Repeat these as much as possible to charge your entire being up and create a you that is a force to be reckoned with.

Journaling about your experiences can help you get to know yourself better. When you know yourself and what you need, you will be more confident. And while it might feel like an illusion at first, it will become true as you begin to believe yourself. Write about what you have experienced and how you felt about it, what you think you did well, and what you learned.

Seek out joy and pleasure in your life. This helps to brighten up your appearance and your overall energy. The more you prioritize your happiness, the more you can create an energy that gets the attention of others. Taking care of yourself and your well-being for a few minutes a day will allow you to show up as a brighter you.

Set boundaries. Find out what you will tolerate in your life and what you will not tolerate. Stick up for yourself. This will help you feel steadier and stronger, which will radiate from your insides to the outside.

Go to therapy. If you have the resources, it can help to go to therapy to get insights into what your behaviors are and how they impact your life. Also, having another person in your life to tell you what you need to know and what you might need to change will help you get to know your patterns. The more you can address things from the inside out, the more it will shift your outer appearance or how you show up to the eyes of others.

But you will notice I didn't say anything about beauty or attractiveness. While these are certainly things people want to change about themselves, there is no one standard of beauty. There is only beauty in being who you are, exactly as you are. Circe teaches this as the one who is just as She is, and She believes others should see it too. And while She was tricked into begging for love, this is not the norm for Her and Her presence in the world.

Purification

Purification can be another act of transmutation and illusion, as well as an honoring of Circe, who purified Jason, Medea, and Odysseus before continuing their journeys.

Some ideas for purification include:

Baths – Taking time to be in a bath can help you remove any spiritual or emotional detritus that can build up from being in the world. You can sink into the water and notice how it allows you to feel unbound by what has held you back or what might be holding you back.

Salt water – Swimming in or anointing yourself with salt water is a common practice for purification too. This can include a whole-body dunk or a few drops on your head or heart to remove what does not serve.

Smoke – Using herbs that are local to your area and not of another culture (again, no white sage, please) to burn for cleansing can be a strong way to not only release yourself from unwanted energies, but also to connect you more deeply in your location.

Wind – If you don't want to use smoke, wind can also be a good way to cleanse your body. You can stand in the wind and allow it to follow the curves of your skin, taking with it anything that does not help you with your goals. Or use a hand fan. Or a box fan.

Cleaning your space – You could also clean the spaces in which you live and work. Taking a few moments to reduce clutter or dust can help you feel more in alignment with the moment and your power. You don't need to do a deep clean. You can remove the clutter and wipe down a few surfaces to get a benefit.

Expanding your magickal practices can be a practice of engaging your imagination to create change. While you may not be able to change what others are doing, you can change how you show up, how you arrive, and what this personal shift can offer to change a situation.

Choosing Ingredients for Spellwork
Note: as with any healing, please check with a doctor before using any herbs internally.

Circe has inspired spellwork for new and old witches. She reminds us that we can conjure our own power and our desires if we are willing and daring. This requires us to tap into who we are and what we already know, even if we don't understand why we know something. You're far more intuitive than you realize. You can sense energy because that's what humans do to protect themselves.

Let's tap into your innate wisdom to choose the best spellwork ingredients. Beyond choosing the right herbs, let's talk more about getting yourself ready to even look at possible herbs. Start by tapping into the feelings of what you want to create in this spell. You can do this by closing your eyes and picturing what you want to have happen because of your magick. Drop into as many senses as you are able: sight, sound, taste, touch, and smell.

- What do you notice when you think about each sense?
- What do you feel in your body when you think about the spell coming to life?
- What emotions come up?
- What stories come up?
- Where do these things feel most alive in your body?

Once you get things to be very clear in your mind and body, you can write things down if that feels helpful, or if you want to continue, here is a practice of calling the ingredients to you.

Calling to the Spell's Desires

Close your eyes and take a few deep breaths. And if you don't want to close your eyes, take a few moments to look around the room to notice what you can sense, e.g., something you can see, hear, taste, touch, and smell. Let this ground you into the space and bring you fully present.

When you are grounded and present, drop away any distractions in your mind. Let them just fall to the ground, away from you and away from your body. Let them disappear, leaving space in your body for something new to arise and become known. You can take as long as you like to let yourself be empty of distraction or as much as possible.

Once you feel free of these distractions, ask yourself what ingredients you need for the spell you need to do. Let anything that comes up be correct and welcome. Just notice what you see, feel, hear, and sense. You might taste something. You might get information that isn't about herbs. You might learn about a chant or a song. Let anything that wants to rise up in your consciousness be witnessed and welcomed.

You can do this for as long as you like. Some people like to ask questions about specific things, e.g., time of day, day of the week, certain rocks, locations, etc. You can be as detailed as you like in this process. The key is to not dismiss anything along the way. Let it all be the right answer.

Once you feel new ideas aren't coming up as much, you can start to come back to the present moment, writing out what you learned. From there, you can do research into what these ingredients are, what they are meant to do, etc. See what resonates and what does not or try everything to see what happens.

What you are likely to notice is that the more you tap into what your inner wisdom has to say, the more it will tell you. Just like any muscle, you can strengthen your intuition with practice and more practice.

Becoming the Sorceress

Hamilton's *Mythology* describes Circe as 'a most beautiful and most dangerous witch," (305). A sorceress is a witch; even if you don't relate to that word, you might want to take that label on after seeing the power of Circe. It is dangerous to know things that can change the world around you.

In my 20+ years as a witch, I have learned that my power has always been with me. I have gained and lost confidence in it over the years, but it was always there and will always be there. I just need to remind myself of what is inherently true from time to time.

And there are ways to call the power back to you. I like to do this as often as possible by closing my eyes and asking my power to return to me from the places it has run off to. When I think of it like a small, curious child that likes to wander, I feel less anxious and more patient when it seems far away.

You can also do a more intensive working to help you come back to yourself. I suggest doing this at a moon phase of growth or fullness, so after a new moon and right up the full moon. However, if the timing isn't right, and you still want to call back your power, you can do this anytime. You can do this every day if you like.

Create sacred space – With any powerful working, it is ideal to create a solid container for magick and to call in allies to support.

Name the obstacles or worries – Once you are surrounded by those who support you and protect you, name the obstacles and worries you have around power. You can talk about specific events or use words or move your body to demonstrate what the lack of power feels like.

Cleanse what does not serve – After you get a clear sense of what is in the way or what is bothering you, cleanse your body from top to bottom. You can do this with water, with incense, with a fan, by shaking or slapping your body, etc. Find a way to dislodge these obstacles from your energetic body. Make sure you are as free of obstacles as you can be. Take your time and do this well and often.

Call to Circe – Once you feel free, call out to Circe to witness that you are ready for your power to come back. You are ready to reclaim what is yours and what has always been yours. Listen and feel when this moment is complete. If it doesn't happen quickly, this is not a bad thing. You might just have to wait longer.

Name your strengths and victories – As you feel your power come back, start to name all of the things you have accomplished and all of the things that make you strong. You can list as many as you like until you feel the energy fill you up from toe to head and everywhere in between.

Create a mantle of power and put it on – As you feel the weight of your own power, you can imagine it beginning to create a mantle or a cloak of energy. Imagine this being put on your shoulders and around your body. This will stay with you. Some like to find a ring or another piece of jewelry to wear daily as a reminder too.

Feel what it feels like – Stop and drop into what this power feels like. What does it feel like to be in your power? What feels different? What feels right? What is a word to describe this feeling?

Thank Circe and close the space – You will know when it's time to stop and end the ritual for now. You can always come back to do this again.

The power you have is always there. You are powerful beyond measure, it's just that the world is often filled with noise to distract you from this truth. While Circe was able to live on an island and not be distracted by outside messaging, you probably need to be in the world and with people. By taking the time each day to remember your power, you can walk with it more easily – in the magick you make and the human you are.

Note:

1. https://www.thegreekherbalist.com/herbalcolumn/ medicinalherbsinancientgreece

Chapter 5

Necromancy & Circe

Necromancy*: conjuration of the spirits of the dead for purposes of magically revealing the future or influencing the course of events; magic, sorcery* (Merriam Webster Dictionary)[1]

Multiple resources connect Circe to being a priestess of Hecate, making a link between this powerful witch and working with the dead. Circe becomes the one who can help Odysseus finally make his way home from Aeaea. He pleaded with this sorceress to make good on Her promise to let him go home one day. She agrees and speaks of how he must take on this journey, including traveling to the underworld to get advice from Tiresias/Teiresias, a blind seer.

Odysseus laid with Circe in her decadent bed, agreeing to a partnership that would benefit each. Odysseus would remain alive, and Circe could have the man She wanted. But as time continued, he wanted to return to his home, and he wanted Circe to make good on her promise to help.

Some translations describe Odysseus making offerings and bowing in supplication to the mighty Circe, reminding her of what she had said when he arrived. He reminds her of the men of his ship and how they have become disgruntled with having to stay on her island while missing their families.

Circe remembered, of course, of the promise and in her power, she is clear that she does not want Odysseus to stay out of some sort of duty. She wants him to stay because he loves Her. Seeing this is not the case, She lets him know he is free to go, but he will need to know of another path that will take him home, but also though the land of Persephone and Hades.

In Her infinite wisdom of the dead, She tells Odysseus to seek the counsel of the spirit of Tiresias, a blind seer. Circe speaks to him of how this wisdom continues to have value in the spirit realm and how Persephone herself has passed it onto the seer. Odysseus is disheartened and cries when he hears this advice. He doesn't know how to travel this way, how to travel to the place of Hades.

But Circe knows the way. She assures him that he needs no pilot or guide as when he raises the mast and spreads the sale, the north wind will take him in the right direction. She tells him that as he sails through the river of Oceanus, he will see a narrow route lined with the tall black poplars of Persephone. He will see the trees and know where to land his boat.

From there, he will need to get out of the boat and follow the stream of Acheron and the entrance to the underworld will be where the waters of Pyriphlegethon meet with a branch of the River Styx. There is a rock there, in the place of where roaring rivers meet. Circe speaks to him of this precise journey and then instructs him on the steps to find the seer. (retelling inspired by Homer, Odyssey 10. 135 – 12. 156, trans. Shewring)

Circe tells Odysseus that he might follow a few steps to get to speak with the blind seer.

1. Dig a trench
2. Surround it with libations – milk and honey, sweet wine, water, barley-meal
3. Offer prayers and sacrifice a ram and a black ewe, bending their heads toward Erebus

The dead require such sacrifices and rituals to know of Odysseus' arrival, and as these are done, he is instructed to turn his head and to look toward the waters of the river. It is then that the dead will arrive to greet the travelers. Circe instructs Odysseus to call to his men to flay and burn the animal sacrifices before praying to Hades and Persephone. Then, Odysseus must wait for the seer to arrive and to reveal the path the ship must take next to find its way home.

Circe offers this willingly as She clearly does not want anyone to stay with Her out of obligation or spite. The way I understand this, She wants him to leave so She knows his return is for Her and not just for what She has to offer in Her wisdom.

Working with the Dead

One of the misconceptions about necromancy is that it is about raising the dead so they can walk among the living again. While this certainly sounds like a (sometimes) useful practice to learn, what is more accurate is that this is the raising of spirits to ask them questions and to offer honor.

Raising spirits can be something you do on certain holidays or everyday practice, depending on the magick you want to have in your life. One can imagine that the spirits of the dead might surround Circe and might have an easier time connecting to them because of Her intense sorcery practice.

For those newer to necromancy, you might start with a few simple practices, following Circe's lead:

Create space for the dead and their memory – The simplest act of remembering and calling to the dead begins with a place for their honor. If you work with dead people you know, this might be as simple as hanging pictures or creating a space of memory. You can then take care of and tend to this space. You can also visit gravesites to honor those who are now in the spirit world.

Offer libations and gifts – Making offerings to the dead is a wise practice, as it honors their gifts, and it focuses on giving back. You can give offerings of drink and food, or you might give special items that specific dead might find favorable.

Make promises – It helps to understand why you want to work with the dead. If you are looking for advice or guidance, you might offer something in return for their help. The promise to tell the stories of the dead or to tend to their resting places are common choices. You might also make specific promises based on what you hear or intuit from the dead as you make room for them.

These are relationships like any other relationship. It takes time for the dead to get to know you and to trust you – and for you to get to know them and trust them. Make small steps to working with spirits. Being consistent will help you connect more deeply and authentically. There are practitioners with resources that can help you, including Mortellus' books, *Do I Have to Wear All Black?* and *The Bones Fall in a Spiral*.

Adding Necromancy to Your Practice

Sitting with spirits to ask them what they have to offer to you can be a simple practice. While there are many complicated practices, starting small will allow you to gain confidence in your necromancy.

I encourage you to sit with the spirit you want to talk to, raising their spirit by making offerings and prayers, and by telling their stories and offering them praise. I think of how I would want to be called back into the world: I would want people to genuinely remember the person I was and the positive things I did in the world. I would want people to call my name and call out to the names they knew me by.

You can sit in a room and do this on your own, or you can work with a group of people. In a group, you might create some sacred space, offer libations, and then call to the spirit you want to raise into the present moment. Having more than one person will often increase the effectiveness of a ritual but know that your singular practice is valid too.

Once you have called the spirit in, as you may have seen in seances and other similar gatherings, you can ask the spirit questions and see what answers arise. This might be that a person in the room becomes filled with the spirit and answers, or the group might just hear and feel things that can be shared aloud.

You can continue to do this practice until the spirit feels as though they are complete in their time with you. This might feel like the group not feeling the presence anymore or that the group doesn't gain any more information from the session.

From there, you will thank the spirit for coming, maybe offer more libations or other gifts, and ask the spirit to go. As a group (or individual), you can then journal about the experience and the wisdom.

Magick of Death and Dying

In my witchcraft tradition, Reclaiming, we reach out to the ancestors and beloved dead during Samhain season. This practice allows the dead to be remembered, and we'll often say, "What is remembered, lives." After all, the dead live on through stories as much as they did in form. These memories allow us to learn and to grow and to know we're never that far away from those who have died.

And there are those who will avoid working with the dead. While I don't dismiss anyone's practice of magick, what I will say is that celebrating and working with death is a part of life and thus a part of magick. There is no love without the reality that everyone will die and lose what they love. There is no rebirth without death. There is no renewal of the Earth without death. Death is part of the turning of the Wheel of the Year. Death is always coming and knowing this can help us live our lives more fully.

I say this because I wonder if Circe reminds us of the magick and death and dying. I have often heard the advice that you cannot heal if you cannot hex. And while I'm not sure that's true for everyone, what does ring true is that knowing how to heal means you also know what is dangerous. Circe makes potions that will turn men into pigs, but those potions do not kill them. She could easily make concoctions to kill someone, and She doesn't make that choice.

Even if it's not the largest part of your practice, I invite you to consider how death and dying might inform your magick. It might be as straightforward as honoring your ancestors or as focused as communing with the dead directly. No matter what you may choose, the acknowledgment of the reality of death can remind you how precious life is.

Remembering that death can be anytime, anywhere, can focus your sorcery in the directions of purpose and power. After all, what do you want to do with the time you have? What might you bring to the world, knowing your time is finite?

Circe has left a legacy of wisdom, power, and transformation, as well as the lessons of anger and its ability to influence actions. What is your legacy?

Note:
1. https://www.merriam-webster.com/dictionary/necromancy

Chapter 6

Circe's Emergence in Culture

I stepped into those woods and my life began,
(Madeline Miller, *Circe*)

Truth be told, Circe seems to be a godd who shows up for people who want to find Her. I'm not sure She was ever in my mind as a goddess to work with until I had been a practicing witch for a while. And even then, I didn't feel She was a being that meant a lot to my personal journey.

After all, I was not out for vengeance at the start of my witch life. I was not interested in turning men into pigs or making potions for illusion. But the ongoing learning about patriarchy and its oppression changed my mind. (As well as Madeline Miller's book, *Circe*.)

Madeline Miller's Influence

When *Circe* came out in 2018, I didn't notice it. I was too busy with other godds, other practices. But soon, the book was shared and recommended across my friend groups. I found the audiobook and listened to it as I walked in my neighborhood; I was altered by the story Miller crafted from Greek myths. I was entranced by how Circe became a being and not just a character.

The book, *Circe*, tells the story of the *Odyssey* from the eyes of Circe. In doing so, this book makes Circe someone who might be seen as completely justified in Her actions. We learn to care about Her after seeing Her be dismissed by Her parents and eventually sent to an island of isolation after confessing to the transmutation of Scylla in Her anger at Glaucus.

Circe is described as having a human voice, though Her eyes were golden and clearly influenced by Her father, the Sun. But She was often seen as being somehow less than Her siblings and out of place. This separation from Her family and Her ongoing desire to be a part of something that didn't want Her sets up the scene for Her desire for power later.

But this book is not about that book. What I want to offer here is the idea that Miller gave readers a chance to get to know a mythological figure in a new way. And while there might be different interpretations of Circe and Her life, this book makes a goddess more accessible and even relatable.

For me, the idea of making a godd relatable is what keeps the godds alive and powerful. When we continue to talk about them and to try to understand them through modern lenses, we create godds that don't die.

At the time of writing this book, Miller's book, *Circe*, had been optioned for a TV series, which was supposed to be released in 2023, at the time of writing.

The (Continued) Rise of the Powerful Woman

With the reversal of Roe vs. Wade in the United States and the ongoing reduction of basic human rights for women in many countries and cities, the powerful Circe is a necessary figure. Not only does She fight back against men, but She also uses magick that can be taught to others. She is not one to suffer fools and She recognizes when helping might be a good decision too.

Circe and other goddesses can become not only figures of influence, but also beings to honor and worship. In that devotion, I must believe we call up the spirits of cunning, discernment, and spell-crafting. The more people we have focusing on these energies, the more effective the magick can be.

The Allure of the Witch and Potions

Of course, there have been plenty of movies and books that centered on the witch who used her knowledge to create potions to change what she didn't like. Remember Sally and Gillian Owens in the *Practical Magic* movie when Gillian tried to make pancake syrup to get rid of the meddling police officer?

The witch has become trendier, and with it, the idea of empowerment. With this trend, moving back to herbalism and making potions to impact our lives is commonplace, almost. While this is certainly not just a Circe influence, we can see how Circe is someone who arrives alongside these magickal tips.

This is all to say that Circe has, interestingly, arrived at a time when the 'bad' witch seems more celebrated than feared. Witches have always been a group of marginalized and oppressed peoples, and Circe can be a figure of inspiration, innovation, and cunning in retaliation. In these times, it is not possible to remain quiet or still on an island; it is necessary to take things into our own hands, to recognize the power of our innate talents and activate change in the world.

Chapter 7

Was Circe Evil?

When I was born, the word for what I was did not exist.
(Madeline Miller, *Circe*)

Because this is likely a question in some minds, I wanted to address it directly: was Circe 'just' evil? After all, the stories we know are about Her anger causing men to become animals. It makes sense that you might be concerned about working with a deity who has not necessarily been the most well-behaved according to modern-day ideas of 'good.'

Defining Evil

If evil is defined as something immoral and wicked, then Circe might fit into that space. Her actions cause harm. She is not someone who forgives easily. And She is someone who consistently does things to punish.

At the same time, She is also someone who loves deeply and longs for someone to love Her. She has children that She adores. According to many stories, Circe changes Her mind on the imprisonment of men in animal forms. In Miller's book, the goddess also seems to have regret about some of Her actions, which is what causes Her to admit to Her wrongs and then be sent to the island to live on Her own. While this isn't a common story, it does add a possibility of this being true.

When looking at translations of any stories, it is wise to consider the translator, as mentioned at the start of this book. While the translator might have the best of intentions, there is a long history of female figures being described as problematic because of their power and their choices.

Looking at Circe, I can see how She could have chosen other methods to handle Her problems, but what about the choices of those who decided to come to Her island without permission or invitation? Would it not be kind and wise to get the approval of Circe (or whoever's island it might be) before settling in and trying to take over the forests?

We also might want to look at how Circe might want to poison Odysseus, but She decides to keep him in Her bed for a year. She further helps him and his men continue their journey, even helping them navigate the underworld and not get pulled in by the Sirens or Scylla. She could have easily let Odysseus get into trouble, but She helps instead, which allows Odysseus to eventually get home after his long journey. You can also see Circe help Jason and Medea, even if it is potentially begrudgingly. She uses the knowledge and wisdom She has to offer them purification as foretold in prophecies.

Alchemizing Anger into Justice

One thing to keep in mind is that energy is energy is energy. Another thing to consider is that stories are not necessarily about their content, and they can act as more of an allegory. What I offer is that Circe is also a symbol and an instigator. She offers the energy of alchemy, turning anger into action. This is an essential lesson in societies where oppressive structures exist and where activism can be unsustainable for some.

I wonder more about how to look to Circe as being a wise teacher about gathering up energy to inform spellwork. I think of Her as also being someone who uses her energy, combined with Her wisdom of herbs, to take on what is unjust. (Even if Her version of unjust may not be one you agree with.)

Emotions are not 'bad' by nature. They are simply pieces of energy that flow through us again and again. They are often heightened by the stories we tell and the people who are involved.

Humans have emotions in a few categories: Fear, Happiness, Sadness, Disgust, Anger, and Surprise. These categories can spread out into more defined words and experiences, but let's stick with what's simple.

Humans have emotions. In this emotional experience, we can decide to act in different directions. When humans can stay emotionally regulated (able to pause before taking action in a situation after considering their experience and their reaction's impact), emotions are not problematic. But when humans are not able to maintain self-awareness, either through a lack of learning or through trauma and other mental health challenges, emotions can incite outbursts, outrage, and damaging consequences. To better work with the power of Circe and learn to utilize these strong emotions for better outcomes:

Make space – Breathe when you feel a strong emotion coming on. Or move your body in another direction. Create space from the feeling, even if you don't know what it is yet. Step back before you step into a response or reaction.

Learn the emotions you have – Using an emotion/feeling wheel to better identify what you are feeling when you are feeling it (I personally like Lindsay Braman's Emotion Sensation Feeling Wheel) will help you slow down to understand what is happening. Once you can name your feelings, you can then decide what you want to do.

Sit with the emotion – Just because you have a feeling doesn't mean you need to act on it. You can wait a few moments (or days) to respond. The more you can sit with an emotion to allow it to be present without trying to fix it or intellectualize it, the more easily you will interact with others in volatile situations. Sitting with the emotion allows it to run through your body and enables you to not feel so intensely since the emotion only stays alive in a body for 90 seconds when you just name it and don't tell a story about it.

Consider what you want in that situation – When you have taken the time to sit with the feeling and reaction, you can then take a breath to see what you want to do. What is the thing that upsets you the most? What action steps can you take? Know that you can hold onto the feeling that you have; anger is quite powerful and inspiring. But you don't have to cause harm and often you don't need to. (I will hedge a little here because I also believe that causing harm is necessary in some situations and it is the best response, e.g., when your safety is threatened, BIPOC and transgender folks' everyday experience, etc.)

Take action – Call up the fires of your anger to keep you going, to keep you moving when things feel overwhelming or unending. I like to create playlists to my emotions so I can pull them back up as needed. I imagine Circe would love an angry playlist. The more you act, the more you build the muscle that emotions can fuel justice and other outcomes. They become allies instead of enemies, accomplices vs. villains.

It is said that anger is one of the most helpful emotions, even if it doesn't feel like it. Anger helps you see where your boundaries have been ignored, even if you let them be ignored. Anger tells you that something isn't right and that you're not safe (or you don't feel safe). The more you listen the more you can see what you need to do to create something better.

I have also heard that anger is sad's bodyguard, and that anger is the outside emotion that protects you from having to feel sadness. If that has resonated with you, it might be wise to stop to think about what makes you also sad about a situation. After all, there are often multiple emotional experiences going on at the same time. By stopping to think about each one, it can help you move your energy in the most effective direction.

Taking action will not get rid of all anger, but it will tell your body that you will respond to anger, which can promote a healthier relationship, one of response instead of reaction.

The Activism That Inspires You

This is the perfect place to talk about the kind of activism that makes the most sense with Circe. This might be the place you expect to see what you are 'supposed' to do when you're working with the goddess. But there are no easy answers with Her and with this magick.

Circe has a clear idea of what is right and wrong in Her life. You can choose to do the same. While I think Circe's magick is aligned with the idea of fighting the patriarchal structures and any oppressive system that seeks to take land or agency away from people, you might find something else.

What you choose to focus on in your magick should be a personal choice, as what you are passionate about is where you will give the most energy. I encourage you to think about what causes make you mad enough to take action. Find groups that are already working on these issues and lend a hand. Find groups online and ask how you can support them. Get to know people in your friend groups that are doing the work and join them.

When it comes to showing up in the streets or in another public way, think about the ways of Circe's magick.

- Herbs to calm tempers and to encourage level-headedness in conflict and violence.
- Spells to decrease/increase visibility. Imagining a cloak of invisibility can help to keep you safe in unknown situations and groups.

- Spells to change your appearance to not be seen or targeted by law enforcement or other oppressive groups. You can call into your body an image of someone who is not catching the eye of anyone. This can extend to any place in which you don't feel safe. You can also do workings like this in groups to help protect events.
- Spells to transform people with bad intentions into 'animals' who are calmer and softer in their interactions. You might have a few animal figures on an altar with Circe to set up the energy that who might threaten you will simply be docile instead.

I might also think about Her ways of seduction and charm. How can these energies be called into your being before challenging events or communications? Can you call on Her to help you better understand the best way forward? Or can you call on Her to tell you what to watch out for? She seems to be a being who knows things ahead of time.

When I say spells, these can be as simple as just calling into your mind what you want to have happen and how you want it to happen. Take time to visualize your desired outcome clearly with all of the senses you can. This will allow you to focus your energy on alchemizing from one possibility to another, fueling something with a desirable result.

The Ethics of Spellcraft

I think Circe can also help us define our own personal ethics and how we make decisions about our actions in the world. By creating your own code of ethics, you can make better decisions in your life and in your magick.

This process starts by finding out what your values are. Put another way, this is what is important to you.

Your values might include Authenticity, Autonomy, Community, Compassion, Creativity, Fairness, Friendship,

Growth, Honesty, Harmony, Justice, Kindness, Love, Loyalty, Peace, Reputation, Respect, Responsibility, Security, Service, Spirituality, Success, etc.

From this list, choose the things that are most important to you in your life. You can add others that might come up. These will help you get a better sense of what is important to you. Once you have that list, you might ask Circe to help you look at it more closely.

- What are the common themes?
- How might these values impact your decision-making?
- How will these impact the way you relate to magick? To other people?
- Are you currently living in alignment with your values?
- What might need to change (or not)?

From this review, you can start to craft an ethics statement that summarizes the kind of person you are and how you strive to act in the world. You do not need to be a perfect person, after all. You can only be the best you can be, and things might change in the future.

But having this list and some sort of statement will help you. When faced with a decision, you can think it through and then look at your values and ethics to see if your solution or action aligns. If not, you can adjust things until things make sense for the person you are and the person you want to be.

What About Hexes and Curses?

The question of whether you should or should not do hexes and curses is what you're probably asking. You might be a person who abides by the threefold law, and the idea that what you put into the world comes back to you three times. While this is perfectly fine for some, I might point out that this often makes it sound like violence or harmful magick isn't useful. It can be for those whose bodies are often the target of harm and violence, e.g., black and brown bodies, transgender folks, queer and nonbinary people, etc.

Though there are many conversations (and arguments) about using left-handed magick or baneful magick, here is what I think: do what you want to do. I'm not going to tell you to do it or not do it. I have done this sort of magick, and I am likely to do it again. However, I will also say that I do seek out alternative magick practices to accomplish what I want to accomplish.

For example, my best example is that I might use an intention of *May you get what you truly deserve.* This allows the universe and godds to decide what that means instead of me directing what harm I want to have happen.

Or I might use the intention of the person seeing themselves as others see them. I've also focused a mirror back on a picture of someone who was being secretive so that their actions and motivations might be seen. Again, these practices don't talk about harming anyone, but rather they focus on letting right-sized things happen to people who are causing harm.

I don't talk about the other kind of work I do because it's done, and it's between me and that working.

Blessings of Circe

To seal the magick of your ethics and your alchemization of emotions, you may want to use this small ritual to witness your working.

Cup of water
List of your values and ethics
Quiet place
Things to honor Circe's presence

Start by creating sacred space in the way you do, e.g., casting a circle, calling elements, etc.

Call out to Circe to aid in your working.

Circe, Sorceress and Witch: I call to you to witness my rite, to honor my magick, and to guide me in my actions. Let this rite be the start of aligned actions and right-sized responses. Support me in this working and I ask for any wisdom you might be able to offer to me.

Read the ethics and values aloud as you hold a cup of water. Notice how the energy of your words sinks into the water. Continue to read your own words until it feels they have completely infused the waters.

Once the water feels 'full,' look into the reflection. Is there anything you can see? Are there any messages in the moment? Can you feel anything? Can you intuit anything?

Offer the cup to Circe and drink the entire cup. Notice how the waters fill you and shift you into a new magick. Notice what you notice around you as you have taken in the power of your own words and your own discernment.

Sit in this space for a few minutes to see if there are any messages that come from Circe.

Once you feel things are complete, thank Circe and close the circle.

Chapter 8

Cultivating a Relationship with Circe

To banish all doubt and distrust you may have in your
power to attract,
look into my eyes. I may be a goddess, the daughter born
to the gleaming Sun; the power of my spells and my herbs
may be great;
but I pray that I may be yours. Reject the one who rejects you,
respond to her who pursues you.
(Ovid, Metamorphoses, 14.32–36)

Deciding to build a relationship with a godd can be the start
of a lifelong collaboration. Not only does working with a deity
help you focus your energy in a certain direction, but it can also
help you expand your awareness of the divine.

When working with Circe, in particular, this can be the start
of a relationship that can expand your power and your ability to
transmute unwanted energies into something else. Hopefully,
the goal is not to turn those you don't like into animals but
transforming that which is unappealing into something more
manageable is a completely ethical goal. (In my opinion,
anyway. Do what you will.)

Know Her

Since you're already at this point of the book, you've started this
step. Getting to know the godd will help you better understand
what they might have to offer you and whether they are the
right fit for your life and magickal goals. I encourage anyone
seeking to build a relationship with any deity to:

- Read books, especially source materials (e.g., *Theogony*)
- Read websites and articles
- Look up images of the deity
- Find art with the deity
- Learn about the culture of their earliest worship, as you can
- Ask questions of experts and scholars
- Take time to sit in silence or meditation with the deity
- Pay attention to signs in your immediate surroundings
- Notice when you see symbols of her, track what you were doing or thinking

Getting to know a deity is much like getting acquainted with anyone. You want to ask questions and listen to what you are told. You also want to consider the sources of the information you receive and whether it is something that rings true for you. Because there is so much information available, it is wise to trust resources that are well-researched.

However, it's also wise to consider the lived experience of those who have worked with the deity, while your experience might differ, it can also help you understand what might be possible. Personal gnosis is just as valid to inform a personal practice, while more researched sources will be best for those seeking to become an expert in what is known about a deity or mythological figure.

I encourage you to start a journal or a note in your phone with the information you learn about Circe. This way, you can see what you have already learned and how that builds on the information you gain in the future. You can also write down your own impressions and feelings about what you learn. By tapping into the body sensations, you will be able to create a somatic experience. This expands your connection beyond what you can learn in a book.

Give to Her

No matter the deity, I encourage you to think about how you can give to the deity you honor. You might choose to set up an altar, for example. Or you might hang a picture of Her on your wall. Or you might set up a dish into which you place offerings that help you give back to the divine.

Offerings were a common practice in ancient Greece, with temples and shrines having places for animal sacrifices and other items. While animal sacrifices are not recommended by this author, you can find ways to bring offerings into your practice with Circe.

In any relationship, the goal is to be reciprocal. After all, deities and people are not gumball machines into which you put a certain point of money (or effort), and you expect to get something in return. Instead, it is best to give what you want to give without expectation of anything in return. This will allow you to establish consistency and trust in the relationship. You are there because you want to be, not because you only want something in return.

There are many ways to give to a deity:

- Herbs and potion ingredients
- Completed potions
- Images of falcons
- Imagines of other animals
- Delicious foods
- Anointing oils
- Art and images of the deity

You might also sense into what Circe wants to see from you specifically. After all, you might have a unique relationship that requires something more and different. You don't have to follow what others have done to be right. It's best to prioritize what you believe to be the best choice, based on what you have learned and what you have gained from time in trance or meditation.

Follow Her

I think it's wise to dive deeper into the stories of Circe to get a better understanding of Her and the way She might impact your life. Reading the stories is the first step, but the next step could be to think about the story from the different views of those in the story. For example, why not look at the story of Circe and Odysseus meeting at first from Her eyes, from his eyes, and then from the eyes of the men. And what do you think the handmaidens thought and experienced?

Think about the motivations of each of the characters if they are clear. Think about how the story might have gone if other choices were made. Think about what would have happened if Circe had turned Odysseus into a pig. Would we have finished his journey? What would have happened to his family?

The more you can follow Her into what is true for Her, the more you can see how this creates complexity and compassion. Even the 'cruelest' goddesses and gods can act in a way that is horrible in the current time, but also be acting in a way that was normal in the time of their first worship.

Think about the time in which Circe was worshipped and written about. What was society like? What was society worried about? What did society fear? What happened to women who had power? What happens to men who were in power? What did the society think of women in general? The more you can follow Her into what is known, the more you will uncover.

In addition, following Her can look like figuring out ways to celebrate and ritualize Her daily. It doesn't have to be anything more than creating a ritual with something you make for a meal every day. Consider the ingredients as pieces of a spell that you are offering to yourself. Think about moving these ingredients intentionally, think about mixing and stirring as magickal and a way to tap into the power of Circe.

You can create small rituals that include reading poetry to Her or singing to Her. If you are able, you might choose to braid your hair to align with the descriptions of Her in the texts. Even if you don't braid all of your hair, a small braid can be a way to hold Her close and help keep Her in mind as often as possible.

I also find that acting out Her stories in my mind can help me better now what Her motivations were or what I think they were. I can also begin to see how She might move in the world, and thus how She might move with me in my life.

Following a deity is a practice that evolves the more you get to know the deity and the more the deity gets to know you. And it is important to say that while you might be asked to do something by a deity, you always have the choice to say yes or no. Or you can find another way to do what is being asked of you. (Better said: you don't have to do an animal sacrifice, but you might offer small bit of meat on an altar or a stuffed animal as a representation.)

Communicate with Her

Circe comes across as a very direct deity, one who does not suffer fools. And that is a great way to live, isn't it? I know I'm inspired by it. It makes sense to work with Her on the ways of communication and directness. This starts with being direct with Her, being consistent in that communication, and finding ways to be direct with yourself.

I encourage you to begin with a daily journaling practice to better understand what is true for you. Figuring this out and documenting it will help you know what you need to communicate – and what you don't need to communicate outside of yourself. Getting to know the inside of your head takes time, but it doesn't have to take hours of each day to get started. The journaling practice can take just a few minutes in the morning and night.

In the morning:

- What am I grateful for?
- What are my goals today?
- How can I support myself today?
- How do I feel about today?

In the evening:

- How do I feel about today now?
- What did I do to support myself?
- How can I do better tomorrow?

You don't need to write more than a few words for each question, collecting what is true for you and tracking what you might be able to do with that information. When you do this, you create a record you can return to see how you have grown and changed. And you can see how when things seemed bad, things eventually shifted to reveal something else.

I find that I need to ask myself direct questions to really get to the heart of what is happening to me on any given day. And while I don't get to journal every day, I do journal fairly consistently, helping my communication stay direct and focused. Because when I can be direct with myself and honest with myself, it will ensure I am more likely to be honest with others.

Communicating with myself is the first step, but communicating with others is next. When I know what I want and what I need, I can express that. I can choose words that will allow a person to understand where I am coming from and how they can respond. While I can't make a person respond in the way I want them to (that's manipulation!), I can be clear about what I want.

Here is a process to ensure you communicate well with others during requests, including Circe:

- What do I need?
- What do I want?
- What can this person/deity do to help me with this?
- When do I need the help?
- What happens if they cannot help me?
- What happens if they say they can and they cannot follow through?

You can practice this process with smaller asks first. This can help you get comfortable with what you need to make requests like this. It might be that you need to write out the answers to all of these questions (or the most relevant ones) until you get used to the practice. And in time, you will be able to take a breath, tap into the questions in your mind, and then ask for what you need immediately.

This work may not seem like magickal work, but boundaries and communication are vital for strong relationships with strong godds. You can't step into a relationship with a godd without a clear sense of what you want and what they can provide. Well, you can do this, but you may not walk away from interactions feeling good about what has happened.

It should be noted that even the most perfect communication can lead to someone saying no to a request. Even the kindest of asks of a person can also be met with anger and defensiveness. The goal of this process is to learn how to communicate clearly and then let go of attachment to outcome. When you do this, you will be able to stay in integrity with your communication. And you'll also learn who you can talk to about certain needs and situations.

I am not saying that Circe will become angry with you for not communicating well, but if you don't have a clear idea of what you want from Her, it is likely you will be disappointed. She wants to help those who are clear about what they need and why they need it from Her. Otherwise, why bother Her on Her island?

To communicate with Circe, you might do the following.

Sit with Her

One of the foundational practices of deity relationships is to start making time for them. This can be as simple as five minutes or as expanded as an hour (or more). The more you relate to the deity, the more you will understand what works best in your unique relationship. At the start, I tend to recommend doing small interactions to get in the habit and to take on a commitment that can be easy to follow.

Meditation – The practice of meditation will help you connect more deeply to the subtle messages of a godd. Start with five minutes of being in silence. This can be sitting, standing, or moving. When you are in this practice, the goal is to keep your mind from getting stuck on unnecessary thoughts. Whenever you feel a new thought come up, you can thank it for being present and then allow it to fade from your consciousness. At first, you will notice many thoughts clamoring for your attention, but in time, they will start to fade and/or become easier to dismiss. As you continue to meditate, you will find your mind is quieter in the rest of the day.

Altar devotion – Building an altar to a deity is a common practice across cultures. How you set this up for Circe might evolve as your relationship does. In most spaces, it helps to have a picture or symbol of the deity to act as a focal point. You might also choose to include some herbs that She has used or herbs you are using in your work with Her. Some find it helpful to have a candle that will be lit whenever you spend time at the altar. Others may find an incense can help to bring more attention to the space, lighting it daily for contemplation. I encourage people working with godds to sit at their altars daily or on a regular basis. Just sitting with the deity and listening to what comes up can build a stronger relationship. You can bring a journal with you to help you track what you have experienced over time. Reading back on these notes can help you better understand how your relationship has growth since the day-to-day can be harder to track.

Write to Her

Circe is a godd who likes good communication, so writing becomes an important practice to consider for working with Her. The more you can reach out to Her and interact with her, the better for your relationship. Be clear in what you want to say and what you want from Her, and this practice will extend to all of your relationships.

Letters to the godds – I have a personal practice of writing letters to the godds, including Circe. You can write to them about what you are experiencing, what you are facing, and what you are needing from Her. This can help you reach out and allow Her response to come at the time it comes. I find it best to write to the godds in a journal and then look around the world at ways you may have gotten answers from Her. And once you have gotten the answer, you can burn the letter, or you can move onto a new question.

Petitions – Another way to reach out about a certain issue is to write a petition to Circe. This doesn't have to be a request for something in return, but it can be. To petition is to request something formally, but you can also petition for the gratitude of a godd. For working with Circe, I might petition for Her wisdom. You can do this by writing what you want on a piece of paper and putting it under a statue of Circe. Or you can put it in a place in nature where you feel She might visit. Again, once you are done with this petition, you can remove it and burn it or you can compost it, if you have that option available.

Candle magick – I think using candles to communicate with godds is an accessible practice. You can write what you want to write to Circe and then light the candle when you want Her to hear it. Some might follow moon phases to help accentuate the message, or you might just light a candle with an everyday intention. Things like "I use my wisdom to protect and heal" or something similar can work perfectly with Circe's energy.

Body messages – Since Circe relates to transmutation, you might also choose to write words for Her on your body. This doesn't have to be a permanent tattoo, rather it can be a few words in a marker or pen to carry the messages to Her. Write a spell on your body where you can only see it or write it out with the tip of your finger so there are no visible words. This will help you change the vision of who you are and can help you walk in the world in a new way. Much like changing into an animal changed the men who Circe transfigured, this practice can help you step into a new way of living.

Interact with Her

Whenever possible, I like to encourage practitioners of all experience levels to find ways to engage with deities in some embodied ways. Instead of keeping your interaction with Circe on an intellectual level, you can bring Her energy into your home and lifestyle. I feel I can get more connected with deities when they are a part of my everyday life, not just my ritual space.

Herbalism – When you are looking to work with Circe as your main deity or as the patron of your magickal practices, taking classes on herbalism would be ideal. You can learn how to make tinctures, potions, and concoctions by working with an expert herbalist. There are also books you can use to learn the basics of working with plants and herbs. I would strongly encourage practice with an in-person teacher to learn the nuance of this practice. And if you are looking to work with any of the herbs mentioned with Circe, it is strongly advised you seek the mentorship of an advanced herbalist to ensure your safety.

Cooking – If you don't want to take on herbalism study, it makes sense to work with Circe in the kitchen. You can connect with Her as you make things from ingredients. With each addition of a new ingredient, you can feel into what it might be like to conjure something new. You can sink into the way that Circe brought together items to offer food to others. Try new recipes from Greece or find ways to improve a recipe from your family to tap into the wisdom that comes from gaining knowledge along the way.

Animal Care – Since Circe is surrounded by animals, you can also connect with Her through caring for animals – yours or not. The more you can attend to animals and their well-being, the more you can begin to see why Circe surrounded herself with these beings. If Circe was able to do such powerful magick, She could have made the choice to kill the men who came to

Her island. But instead, She chose to change them into animals, surrounding Herself with living, breathing beings.

Weaving – When Odysseus arrives on the island of Circe, She is described as weaving, likely at a loom, and singing sweetly. This image of Her might sound like a domestic setting, but it was common for women to weave during ancient Greece and highly valued. You don't necessarily have to get a loom or spin your own yarn, but you can braid or plait yarn. Or you can knit or crochet with Circe to see what it feels like to be in this act of creation with a godd. You could weave something and weave magickal intentions into the pattern.

Playlists – As you get to know Circe better, you might be able to pick out music that She might like or music that might inspire Her energy. You can build playlists to use in your magick with Her or to dance with Her during devotional work. I find playlists helpful for getting into trances more easily. Moving my body to a playlist will often be my meditative practice, with me moving until I feel Her presence and then slowing to listen to what arrives in this moment. You might choose to create playlists for Her anger, Her power, and Her gift with plants.

Dream with Her
Working with a deity during dreamtime is something that I would suggest for Circe too. Since She is a goddess who has worked with drugs that produce hallucinatory states, moving into dream land seems a reasonable connection point.

Create a dream bag – If you can, you can create a small bag with dreaming herbs or herbs that you associate with Circe. This bag might be placed under your pillow or placed in your clothing when you go to bed each night. This will anchor you to the dream working and it can help you remember dreams more easily.

Dream incubation – Researchers note that forms of dream incubation have been around for 5000 years across cultures.[1] While the methodology has changed, this practice has helped build stronger relationships to the divine. What you can do is become quiet before your bedtime and drop into what you want to learn from your dreams. This can be a question for Circe directly or for the magick that She can create. Once you have this question in your mind, ask yourself and Circe to focus on this question during the time you are asleep. You can also specifically say that you will remember what you need to remember in the morning. Some people like to write down their intention before bed, and then write what they learned under that intention when they awake in the morning.

When you are attempting to build and cultivate a relationship with Circe, I encourage you to think about the being She is and how you can relate to those qualities. You might find there are other activities She wants to do with you. And if that is the case, you can always follow Her guidance to see what that might offer.

Invite Her into You

Aspecting is a practice of possession in which you can take the energy of a deity into your body, offering them a vehicle in which to experience the present day. When I teach this practice in Reclaiming Witchcraft classes, I advise people not to do this practice on their own, at least not at first. But if you are a person that doesn't have a coven or a working magickal group, there are still ways to tap into possession work in a safe way.

Since there are different levels of aspecting, you can choose to have a lighter experience, though no less powerful and helpful.

One of the levels of aspecting is 'inspired,' which means you are influenced by the spirit of the deity though not overcome by it. You can do this in a few ways. Some like to become still in their bodies and imagine the deity resting on their shoulders, influencing thoughts and actions of the one who has called the deity over for a visit.

You can also take a cloth and breath Circe's energy into it, putting it on your shoulders to take on Her energy, but then be able to take the cloth off when you are done. In addition, you could also hold onto an altar item that represents Her, and then envision Her energy coming up your arm and into you. Once done, you can put the item down.

When you have the energy of Circe in you, you might ask questions, or you might just sit with Her to see what She has to say or do. It can help to have questions prepared ahead of time, especially when you're first getting to know Her. Then, either in the aspecting or when you're done, write out the answers to the questions.

You can also just journal or record what you have to say when you're in aspect. This can be contained with an alarm to remind yourself of the time container you will use and when the deity will leave you. I was taught that body always trumps spirit, so you can tell the deity when to go and they will leave. There is no need to worry that a deity will get 'stuck' in you.

It is wise to have an altar set up for the deity ahead of time and to have the space be free from any distractions so you can easily step into – and hold onto – the energy.

The act of aspecting is a devotional act and can be a vital part of building a relationship with a deity. You can often get information from this practice that you would not (and could not) get from a book.

Dedicating to Circe

To dedicate yourself to Circe is to step into a relationship with a powerful being. This godd is not only vengeful and wise, but She is also able to take care of herself no matter what comes

Her way. While She may not always make decisions modern society would agree with, it is clear She is someone who does take action.

She does not hesitate. She knows what to do next, how to do it, and when to step in. She is a lover, and She loves, She is a healer and a hexer. She is a force to be reckoned with and Circe can teach you about power.

You will need:

Altar to Circe
An invocation/prayer to Circe – why do you want to dedicate to Her?
Food
Drink / libation
Three herbs that make you feel powerful and wise
A bowl of water

If you can for this ritual, it would be nice to be outside in nature, as though on the island with Circe. But if you cannot, you can also take time to think about what the forest of Aeaea looks like to you in your mind. Close the door to the room you are in and know yourself to be there.

Set up an altar to Circe, with images, item, and other things you think She'd like. You can put this altar in the middle of the ritual space or off to the side, depending on your preference. Put the food and drink on here too.

Begin by creating sacred space. I would include a cleansing, grounding, and circle casting to ensure the best possible container. Take your time with this. This is not a time to rush into magick.

Once the space feels sacred, call out to Circe with the invocation or prayer you have created. Take your time to make sure She hears not only the words, but also the emotions behind those words. Let the words hang in the air for a little bit before moving onto the next part.

Take the bowl of water and remember it as the spell of connection from that prior chapter. Take a look at your reflection in that water. See how you are powerful just as you are, and you are worthy of stepping into more power with Circe as a guide.

Into the water, place the herbs that you have chosen for power, speaking about each herb as you add it to the water. Stir this around clockwise at least three times. Once the water and herbs are stirred, think about what the water contains and how you have created it. You have chosen this potion based on your intuition and wisdom.

At this point, you have a few options, you can choose to disrobe, or you can make a part of your skin more available. You are going to anoint yourself or bathe yourself in this water and herb mixture. This will help you take in your intention by offering it to the largest organ of your body.

You can choose the place where the water goes and how it will be placed there. You might want to focus on your heart, your hands, your head, etc. This part is up to you. Maybe you want to put the water on the places that align with your intentions. Or maybe you want to put the water on the places that feel like they need more power.

Once you have anointed yourself and used up all the water, turn to Circe's altar and ask that She witness you in your dedication. Ask for Her blessing and ask for Her strength. You might commit yourself to a year and a day, with the idea you will renew this commitment if it feels right at that time.

Allow yourself to feel the power of Circe on your shoulders, the power of the great enchantress along your skin. This magick is waking up inside you already. You are going to be working together and let the magick begin in this moment.

Whenever you feel ready to be complete, and there is no rush, take some of the food and drink and offer it to Circe. Then take some of the food and drink for yourself, allowing yourself to ground down into the magick you have created together.

Take the time you need here too. Once you feel complete, thank Circe for all that She is and all that She might become in your life. Open the circle and clean up.

Note:

1. http://www.dreamscience.ca/en/documents/New%20 content/incubation/Incubation%20overview%20for%20 website%20updated.pdf

Conclusion

Circe, I call to you,
Circe, I call to your power,
Circe, I call to your wisdom,

I call to the way of transmutation
That shifts what needs to be changed
I call to the way of illusion
That hides what needs to be hidden
I call to the way of necromancy
That connects me to the wisdom of the dead

I ask you to help me take my anger to fuel my magick
I ask you to help me in seeing the best action
I ask you to help me know the next step

With your wisdom of herbs and potions
I call myself into the spell
With your knowledge of animals
I call myself into the spell
With your trust in your self
I call myself into the spell

May your sorcery inspire me
May your magick fuel me
May your power remind me
That I too can be dangerous

Circe, you are rightfully feared
Circe, you are rightfully blessed
Circe, you are welcome to my life

While Circe has a reputation wider than the distance between Her island and Her home, She offers power and wisdom to all who make the journey. When you begin to listen to what She has to say and what She has to share, you can see how Her energy is fitting for the ongoing and insidious oppression of the patriarchy.

The image of turning men into pigs is the one that will stick out the most when it comes to Circe. She does not suffer fools. She does not wait for advice or counsel. She does what She thinks is best and does step back when needed. She does offer Her talents when they will come in handy. She will support family and children and She will change Her mind.

I invite you to turn to Circe to sit with Her and to follow Her to the island where animals surround Her. Step into the place of power that knows Her name and offers the potions that can harm and heal. Step into the magick that is fierce and angry, and just the right size for the battles for justice in this world.

Appendix A – Resources

Hesiod, *Theogony* Translated by M.L. West

LeFae, Phoenix. *Witches, Heretics & Warrior Women: Ignite Your Rebel Spirit through Magick & Ritual*

Mankey, Jason & Taylor, Astrea. *Modern Witchcraft with the Greek Gods: History, Insights & Magickal Practice*

Miller, Madeline. *Circe*

Trzaskoma, Stephen, Smith, M. Scott, and Burnet, Stephen, edited and translated by. *Anthology of Classical Myth: Primary Sources in Translation* second edition

Weigle, Marta. *Spiders and Spinsters: Women & Mythology*

Yarnall, Judith. *Transformations of Circe: The History of an Enchantress*

Appendix B – Bibliography

Books

Baring, Anne and Cashford, Jules. *The Myth of the Goddess: Evolution of an Image*

Homer. *The Odyssey* Translated by Robert Fagles

Kerènyi, Karl. *Goddesses of Sun and Moon*

Lefkowitz, Mary R. *Women in Greek Myth* Second edition

Monaghan, Patricia. *The New Book of Goddesses & Heroines*

Pomeroy, Sarah B. *Goddesses, Whores, Wives, and Slaves*

Digital Resources

https://www.toledoblade.com/news/deaths/2004/06/05/Toledo-witch-founded-church/stories/200406050050

http://circleofthesacredgrove.org/honoring-lady-circe/

https://witchingphilosophical.wordpress.com/2016/05/30/lady-circe/

https://theweek.com/articles/872174/what-happens-when-women-translate-classics#:~:text=Among%20the%20early%2Dmodern%20women,respected%20Classicists%20of%20her%20time.

https://www.34st.com/article/2019/10/emily-wilson-penn-classical-studies-translation-the-odyssey-macarthur-foundation-genius-grant-fellowship#:~:text=Two%20years%20ago%2C%20Penn's%20Classical,Homer's%20The%20Odyssey%20into%20English.

https://heroesjourneyssummer2017.wordpress.com/2017/07/21/the-odyssey-and-the-heros-journey/

https://en.wikipedia.org/wiki/Circe

https://www.britannica.com/topic/Circe-Greek-mythology

https://www.theoi.com/Titan/Kirke.html

https://greekreporter.com/2023/01/02/circe-witch-greek-mythology/

https://www.greeklegendsandmyths.com/circe.html
https://www.thecollector.com/circe-sorceress-odyssey/
https://www.storynory.com/circe-the-beautiful-witch/
https://owlcation.com/humanities/The-Sorceress-Cerce-in-Greek-Mythology
https://www.hellenicaworld.com/Greece/Mythology/en/Circe.html
https://www.in2greece.com/english/historymyth/mythology/names/circe.htm
https://study.com/learn/lesson/circe-odyssey-summary-myth.html
https://mythologyexplained.com/circe-in-greek-mythology/
https://www.faculty.umb.edu/gary_zabel/Courses/Phil%20281b/Philosophy%20of%20Magic/Pythagoras,%20Empedocles,%20Plato/Circe,%20Greek%20Mythology%20Link.htm
https://mythologysource.com/circe-greek-goddess/
https://mythus.fandom.com/wiki/Circe
http://www.mythencyclopedia.com/Ca-Cr/Circe.html
https://classicalwisdom.com/mythology/monsters/circe-justice-for-the-witch/
https://www.worldhistory.org/Circe/
https://www.ancient-origins.net/myths-legends-europe/spellbinding-story-circe-goddess-magic-006787
https://www.greekmythology.com/Other_Gods/Circe/circe.html
https://greekgodsandgoddesses.net/goddesses/circe/
http://www.dreamscience.ca/en/documents/New%20content/incubation/Incubation%20overview%20for%20website%20updated.pdf
https://womeninantiquity.wordpress.com/2023/03/28/depictions-of-circe-throughout-the-ages/
https://www.biblicalarchaeology.org/daily/ancient-cultures/daily-life-and-practice/ancient-necromancy/

https://www.learnreligions.com/what-is-necromancy-4796625
https://www.thegreekherbalist.com/herbalcolumn/medicinal
  herbsinancientgreece

About the Author

Irisanya Moon is a priestess, teacher, and initiate in the Reclaiming tradition. She has taught classes and camps around the world, including in the US, Canada, UK, and Australia. Irisanya writes a regular blog, *Charged by the Goddess*, for Patheos, as well as a Substack newsletter called Heart Magick, which can be found at https://irisanya.substack.com/

You can find out more about Irisanya's writing and teaching at...
www.irisanyamoon.com

You can find her blog at...
https://www.patheos.com/blogs/chargedbythegoddess

Books by Irisanya Moon...

Earth Spirit
Gaia: Saving Her, Saving Ourselves
Honoring the Wild

Pagan Portals
Reclaiming Witchcraft
Aphrodite
Iris
The Norns
Artemis

Practically Pagan
An Alternative Guide to Health & Well-being

MOON BOOKS
PAGANISM & SHAMANISM

What is Paganism? A religion, a spirituality, an alternative
belief system, nature worship? You can find support for
all these definitions (and many more) in dictionaries,
encyclopaedias, and text books of religion, but subscribe to
any one and the truth will evade you. Above all Paganism is
a creative pursuit, an encounter with reality, an exploration
of meaning and an expression of the soul. Druids, Heathens,
Wiccans and others, all contribute their insights and literary
riches to the Pagan tradition. Moon Books invites you
to begin or to deepen your own encounter,
right here, right now.

If you have enjoyed this book, why not tell other readers by
posting a review on your preferred book site.

Readers of ebooks can buy or view any of these bestsellers by clicking on the live link in the title. Most titles are published in paperback and as an ebook. Paperbacks are available in traditional bookshops. Both print and ebook formats are available online.

Find more titles and sign up to our readers' newsletter
www.collectiveinkbooks.com/paganism

For video content, author interviews and more, please subscribe to our YouTube channel.

MoonBooksPublishing

Follow us on social media for book news, promotions and more:

Facebook: Moon Books

Instagram: @MoonBooksCI

Twitter: @MoonBooksCI

TikTok: @MoonBooksCI